AF893721

The Greatest Legacy

Sharing Our Faith With Our Grandchildren

Pat Parker

Dace Publishing
Ruckersville, Virginia

Scripture quotations in this book are from the following sources:

Scripture taken from *The Holy Bible, New International Version.* Copyright © 1973, 1978, 1984 by International Bible Society. Used by permission of Zondervan Publishing House. All rights reserved.

The Holy Bible, New Century Version (NCV). Copyright © 1987, 1988, 1991 by Word Publishing, Dallas, Texas 75234. Used by Permission.

The Holy Bible, New King James Version (NKJV). Copyright © 1982, 1994 by Thomas Nelson, Inc., Nashville, Tennessee. Used by Permission.

The Living Bible, (TLB) Copyright © 1971 by Tyndale House Publishers, Wheaton, Illinois, 60187.

The Holy Bible, Revised Standard Version (RSV). Old Testament Section, Copyright 1052; New Testament Section, Copyright © 1946 by the Division of Christian Education of the National Council of Churches of Christ in the United States of America. Published in New York by Thomas Nelson and Sons.

The Scripture quotations herein from the *New Revised Standard Version Bible,* (NRSV) Copyright © 1987 by the Division of Christian Education of the National Council of Churches of Christ in the U.S.A. are used by persmission.

*The Jerusalem Bible:*Copyright © 1966 by Darton, Longman & Todd,Ltd., and Doubleday & Company, Inc.

The New Oxford Annotated Bible with Apocrapha (NOAB/NRSV). Copyright © 1991by Oxford University Press, Inc. New York.

The King James Version of the Bible (KJV).

Copyright 2000 by Pat Parker
All rights reserved. This book, or parts thereof, may not be reproduced in any form without express written permission.

Published by Dace Publishing
P.O. Box 91, Ruckersville, VA 22968

Printed in Canada

ISBN 0-932045-39-1
Library of Congress Catalog Card Number 00-131216

First Edition, 2000

These words are dedicated to all little children everywhere,
to all grandparents who find true joy
in their grandchildren.
and
especially to our Jessica, Dylan, and Parker.

To my family, John,Rochelle, John W., and Angela
To friends, Joy and Mary
Deep love and gratitude for your support and assistance

For Oak Grove, my childhood church
For Central, my present church
and for the many churches between these as we lived in the world
I will be forever thankful.

How to Order This Book

Copies of this book may be ordered from:

Dace Publishing
P.O. Box 91
Ruckersville, VA 22968
(888) 840-DACE (3223)
FAX (804) 985-4577

- Order by phone, FAX, or mail.
- Please include quantity and title, along with name, address, phone number and shipping address if different from order address.
- Payment must accompany order.
- $ per copy, plus $3.00 shipping/handling
- Checks or Money Orders should be made out to Dace Publishing
- If ordering with VISA/MC/AmEx, please include name of cardholder, card number and Ex. date.

Groups, schools, chruches, or organizations interested in ordering this title in quantity, please contact Dace for quantity discounts.
Trade discounts available.

- Pat Parker is available for speaking to groups on this topic. Please call Dace Publishing for more information.

- Contact Dace Publishing for other available titles.

If you are a writer, Dace is interested in discussing your title and interests. We work with developing authors in a number of different ways as well as established authors with good material.
Please contact us for more information at
(888) 840-DACE (3223)

CONTENTS

Foreword

My wife and I first became aware of the idea of "legacy" when our school-aged daughters informed us at the supper table that we were "the only family they knew who still sat down for a meal together every night." As we talked, we discovered their friends' parents felt lucky if they even saw their children for one or two meals a week. We also learned our daughters' peers were seldom taught or given examples of moral virtue or spiritual growth in their homes. My wife and I were surprised, because we knew these parents were all prominent members of the community. It warmed our hearts, however, when our younger daughter ended the discussion with, "I'm glad we have Christian parents who care about us."

Although I'm her pastor, I do not view Pat Parker as "just a parishioner." I see her as a fellow faith pilgrim and a co-worker in Christ. She speaks of issues of faith from her own experience. Her words carry a strong moral authority that give readers a broader understanding of our need to pass our faith on to younger generations, all of which comes from participating in and learning through the faith community. We look to Pat for leadership in our own congregation, especially in the areas of Christian nurture and the cultivation of Christian families. She has helped us learn that the word "family" carries a broader meaning in the Christian community. As Christian adults, each of us is blessed with the opportunity to nurture all of God's children.

In *The Greatest Legacy* Pat offers grandparents an opportunity to "love, pray, and live out their faith in front of and with their grandchildren" Her method of commentary, coupled with practical application, will equip any loving grandparent with the spiritual tools they need to touch their grandchild's soul. We need grandparents to bridge the growing spiritual generation gap that plagues our society and our families. Pat's use of the words "intentional, committed, and sacred work" remind us of God's call to action. Your grandchildren—and yes, your children—need your wisdom and example.

Parents, teachers, pastors, and any adult who wants to be a positive presence for the children of their community should read and apply this book to their experience. It could serve as a study guide for groups who want to provide a Christian example for children in their churches and neighborhoods. Many children around us lack grandparents, either by distance or circumstance, and they have a special need for "adopted grandparents."

To offer a legacy implies that we are to reach into a rich, meaningful past to offer gifts for the present and hope for the future. Grandparents should offer a great spiritual legacy to their grandchildren. As a part of her legacy, Pat Parker offers us this powerful and important book.

Phillip B. Cole, pastor
Central United Methodist Church, Mt. Airy, North Carolina

The Greatest Legacy

Sharing Our Faith With Our Grandchildren

Introduction

All Children Need Adults

"The world has yet to see what God can do
with and for and through
a [grandparent] who is fully consecrated to Him."
Henry Barley, Irish preacher more than a century ago.

This book is written for grandparents who are uneasy about the effect the continuing spiritual and moral deterioration has on their grandchildren. Even in the best situations, young children are at risk daily because of the social environment in which they must live.

We're deluged by media's explicit language and depictions of violence; all of it offensive to anyone whose sensibilities still can be shocked, and certainly to children. If television at home is never turned on in their presence, even then it is impossible to protect children from the onslaught of potentially damaging images projected into their minds and emotions.

Time away from home for school-age children is greater than their time awake with their families. At school, friends share stories of children who bring guns to murder their classmates, of youth suicides, of childhood abductions, and other daily atrocities. They know many children in their classes who use drugs, and some who live in violent homes. The relationships of many adults in their lives are often violent, strange and scary, short-lived and disposable. Life all about them is unlike anything we ever experienced in our childhood.

Many grandparents have caring relationships with their grandchildren and the children's parents, providing stability for their lives. There is good communication and shared companionship as the children in these families are showered by unconditional love; however, some grandparents go to bed each night dreading the next morning's news, praying that their grandchildren will not be a part of it.

We may prevent, or heal, the disorder in our young families and bring hope and spiritual health to our grandchildren by sharing our faith with them in ways that enlighten and enhance their lives. Without belief in God as guidance for their daily lives, the scariness, dismay, lack of direction, and lack of hope may overwhelm them to despair.

**The message that tells of God
must be delivered anew to each generation,
and grandparents are called to be the messengers.**

We know God's love changes our lives when we acknowledge His presence and follow His guidance; however, we may be withholding knowledge of His grace and the power of His goodness from our grandchildren if we are not overtly communicating this to them. We'll enrich our grandchildren's lives by portraying Christ and living as God guides us in all we do. Let's ask God to help us share our faith with our grandchildren during the following months.

*"In you our fathers put their trust,
they trusted and you delivered them."*
Psalm 22:4 (NIV)

For many grandparents, this experience may be accomplished only through committed determination and with great difficulty. The composition of today's families is significantly different from that of our own families as we grew up. Some grandchildren live in one-parent homes, foster homes, two-parent one-sex homes, abusive and negligent homes, jails, shelters for runaways, or on the streets. Wherever they're living, each one is, or was, someone's grandchild and their grandparents can bring about changes in their lives.

Our grandchildren may live in secure, happy homes with parents who have goals for themselves and their children. They may live near enough to us that we see them daily, or so far away that we see them only annually. This book may be used in any way which you may devise to help your grandchildren wherever they are, or whatever their circumstances, to learn about and become involved in the faith of their families. Use letters and packages, phone calls, e-mail, frequent visits to them, long summer visits with you, or other innovative measures to reach them. You may also tell their parents or substitute parents about this book so they may participate in the plan you develop.

The following chapters are designed to challenge and guide us in helping our grandchildren experience our Christian strengths. We may proceed as slowly as needed, skip about in the book, fit our plans to the specific ages and needs of our grandchildren, and add our own knowledge and innovations.

In Proverbs we're reminded through King Solomon's words: *"When a good man dies he leaves an inheritance to his grandchildren."*

Is it possible to give our grandchildren any greater gift than the gift of faith?

This book omits specific dogma, doctrinal matters, and directed religious practices. Inclusions regarding each grandparent's personal faith may be incorporated as we wish. The content enhances the beliefs we hold already, and it encourages further study that we may more fully provide the spiritual needs of our individual grandchildren.

"Whether you turn to the right or to the left,
your ears will hear a voice behind you, saying,
'This is the way; walk in it.'"
Isaiah 30:21 (NIV)

"Then I heard the voice of the Lord saying,
'Whom shall I send? And who will go for us?'
And I said, 'Here am I. Send me!'"
Isaiah 6:8 (NIV)

Why Grandparents Are So Critically Needed

"He gives strength
to those who are tired
and more power to those who are weak."
Isaiah 40:29 (NCV)

The disintegration of America's families is a social problem which is compounding from generation to generation. When parents fail their children, there is little the children of that generation have to pass on to their own children. This failure compounds negligence, poverty, abuse and violence, and other sociological ills—and, most detrimental to these children, spiritual deprivation.

Failure-to-live-righteously is the climate in which we now live. We may recognize the spiritual void around us, while doing little to change our own lifestyles. Instead of being change agents, we too often tread the path of materialism while promoting our we-must-feel-good-all-the-time society by finding more ways and places to entertain our grandchildren. We buy more unneeded things for them and allow more indulgences. We realize materialism is a social illness; however, we often relate love to material gifts instead of giving of ourselves more fully.

Grandparents may be inspirational examples for their grandchildren by responding to them with attitudes of gratitude, tranquility, and support while participating in non-materialistic activities.

A relationship built on conversations,
secretive plans to surprise another family member,
solving problems, cooking, gardening, sharing chores,
making and carrying out goals, playing games or
working on other activities which may be shared
will be cherished for a lifetime.

Let's encourage our grandchildren to recognize God's presence in their lives and allow them time to think and experience life, to be quiet and still—alone, or with us—to wonder and dream, to think of the good in their lives, and to sense God's nearness. When we do this they may soon come to cherish these times.

Most of today's working parents are rushed in everything they do; consequently, any time and energy they have left for their children is mostly perfunctory. Feeling they're expected to overextend themselves, these young parents put more into their hours than is sensible or healthy, adding guilt to the already present overload. Guilt causes us all to pour on extravagances in many areas of life as we try to make up for our inadequate caring.

Parents may neglect to see the real needs of their children. Today there's more need for parental time to be spent with children than in any previous generation because there are fewer trustworthy adults outside the family. In our active, complicated world, potential danger in many forms looms over young children. Life is much more frightening for our grandchildren than it ever was for us. We see many children behaving as adults in children's bodies—their childhood put aside, never to be retrieved. Because of our social climate more trustworthy and reliable adult availability, and adult hands-on assistance, is needed by most children.

Today's Faith Is a Private Matter

"For if you remain silent at this time,
relief and deliverance . . . will arise from another place,
but you and your father's family will perish."
Esther 4:14 (NIV)

Many young parents are reluctant to mention their religious beliefs or God at their jobs, to casual friends, or at formal or informal gatherings. They're infected by the secular contagion that causes people to "shut up about religion" and to keep all mention of their faith private. Their family life is compartmentalized: church is for God, and everything else is secular. In this climate, criminals are heroes, to be greedy is sensible—even admirable, compassion for others is a nuisance, and truth is anything anyone calls it.

Teaching religious topics isn't permitted in public schools; therefore, many children have little exposure to the faith of their ancestors. Federal laws are upheld which protect our children from being exposed to religion in their schools. The Constitution of the United States of America provides for separation of church and state. We know what our founding fathers intended by this, but at no time should these words be interpreted to mean separation of our country's leaders or any others from religious faith or Christian discipleship.

**We're living in an age of secularization,
in a culture that proclaims
the fast-paced, materialistic, proficient world around us
will provide our needs,
protect us from harm, and secure our futures.**

We're informed that products satisfy, college degrees and the government will guarantee income, and happiness can be bought; but realistically, many families feel emotionally and spiritually dead in their longing for an unidentified satisfaction.

For too many, personal greed has come to be an honorable goal and showing concern for those who are less fortunate is not a priority. Instead, the needs of others are often ignored; or worse, the needy are denounced with blatant hostility. The overriding consideration of the ego-centered individual of our times is for his own wants, not for others' needs. We are no longer our brother's keeper.

The plight of our children is not honestly acknowledged by our society of hardened hearts. Declaring interest in our nation's children is uttered most often to produce votes. Our courts are desensitized to abuse and violence to such an extent that criminals who steal cars are often given harsher sentences than one who murders his own child.

In this atmosphere, where so many concerns come between young parents and their children, many grandparents reluctantly perceive their adult children as having abandoned their earlier religious training. These young parents are struggling to meet daily demands and find no time for the inclusion of religious involvement in their families' lives.

Yes! We're critically needed.

The wisdom of theologians, teachers, and psychologists clearly warns us that a spiritual life of some kind is necessary for our overall health and well-being. It's time for us to help our children and their children, time to conscientiously reinstate the practice of religion in our homes and teach our grandchildren the beliefs of our ancestors. Let's remember these words from Joshua, *As for me and my household, we will serve the Lord.*

We can be messengers of hope for our families. We have the time, the resources, the wisdom, the depth of our faith, and the love of God needed to make the difference.

"And who knows, [we] may have been chosen . . .
for just such a time as this."
Esther 4:46 (NIV)

How We Can Make a Difference

"Without the Divine assistance, I cannot succeed;
with it, I cannot fail."
Abraham Lincoln

As grandparents, we have influential connections to our grandchildren which no other adults have. This relationship, which is ours alone, is uniquely special. Our love engulfs them and binds us tightly to them. We all love our grandchildren and want the best of everything for them. We hurt when we learn they're hurting or are deprived.

We want our grandchildren to experience the blessings God provides in their times of joy and sadness, loneliness and temptation. We'll help them know God's love is available to them and that He will comfort them when they are troubled. Our years of living in faith and our deep trust in God is our treasure to share with them; it will provide more for them than any material gift. Think of the massive reserves of unused spiritual resources you have available to benefit your grandchildren and their parents.

Most grandparents have special talents and unusual experiences with which to enrich grandchildren's lives—artistic and crafts talents, musical abilities, love and knowledge of nature, outdoor and indoor sports, stories of places you've been and things you've done. Add your adeptness at needlework, crossword puzzles, interests in history, literature, archaeology, astrology—all this is who we are. We are made up of all our interests and abilities, our knowledge, and our innermost longings. These are a part of our spiritual identities. Sharing these in the light of our faith will make most of our times together both enjoyable and memorable. Some, through your love and your devotion to your faith, are already involved spiritually.

In addition to enjoying our times together, let's be committed to exemplifying Christian behavior and attitudes when we're with our grandchildren. It's the living we do that influences younger generations. Through this we may impact their futures and, very possibly, the futures of their children.

Whatever time we spend with our grandchildren portraying our Christian faith may be the only glimmer of spiritual enlightenment our grandchildren have available to them on this day.

Our grandchildren need our help now. None of us are self-made. We often needed others as we grew in faith. We owe our parents, and all our ancestors—and we owe the circuit riders, our ministers and Sunday School teachers, and the Christian fellowship of our churches; we are indebted to the woman next door who first took us to church, and many others who helped us become the persons we are. We didn't find our faith by ourselves. Prayers, watchful guided assistance, encouragement, weekly religious education, and loving care by vast numbers of caring adults (many of whom we're unaware) brought us to this day. This same support is being denied many grandchildren today.

Being a grandparent is not an insignificant state of being. When grandchildren don't have the grandparent relationship of unconditional love, they're denied one of the richest bonuses life has to offer. Let's deepen this relationship by introducing our grandchildren to God's love, His forgiveness and guidance, the joy of His creation through nature, and His special care for children by placing them within families. This will be an abiding enhancement to their lives, and to ours.

"May the favor of the Lord our God rest upon us;
establish the work of our hands for us—yes,
establish the work of our hands."
Psalm 90:17 (NIV)

Making Up for Times Past

"Trust in the Lord with all your heart, and lean not on your own understanding."
Proverbs 3:5 (NIV)

Why should we grandparents be responsible for our grandchildren's spiritual lives? Because, in many cases, we ourselves may have been negligent. Perhaps we unknowingly failed our own children. Did we overemphasize the work ethic and slight the importance of our Christian faith when they were growing up?

Many grandparents sense a missing dimension in their adult children's homes. There are no prayers, no Bible in evidence and no verbal expressions of Christian faith. And, too few attend church and Sunday School. As our children were growing up, the attitudes and practices regarding our faith may have closely resembled the ones currently seen in these homes.

Our adult children are good, loving, hard-working, and seriously capable parents. However, during the past few years they've become easy targets, being unfairly blamed for all that's wrong with our nation's children; consequently, they feel responsible for any difficulties in their families and are working more to enhance their family life than we ever had to work. They teach their children society's basic values and the best ethical behaviors; however, we realize something is missing.

Ethics and manners and kindness to others can be taught without using a Bible, mentioning God or Jesus, or attending worship services at church.

Our families are not anti-Christian, nor do they deny God's existence. They simply have become secularized to the point of living without acknowledgment of God. There is no recognition or spoken words relating to their religious heritage, or to their spiritual existence; nor is there any overt gratitude to God for His gifts, graciousness, and His continued closeness to them.

**God is available to us,
even in our negligence of Him.**

Most children are not informed of the origination of the ethics guiding them: The Ten Commandments, and Jesus' teaching. They're learning to be good, well-mannered children and good citizens merely for the sake of being good, or for some other secular reason related to monetary or social payoff in the future.

The absence of faith stories, of relating personal experiences, of reading the Bible together as a family, and of praying together, is the same absence that may have occurred in many of our homes as our children were growing up. We acknowledged our Christian faith, but perhaps we neglected the teaching that would have inspired them into their adulthood.

We went to church and took our children. They participated in Sunday school with their friends while we sat in adult classes and in worship services. We attended church meetings, helped raise money, held offices—all with our friends. Our church attendance may have been seen as a social outing by our children, rather than Christian witness.

When we disagreed with the behavior and ideas of our children's friends and their plans, seldom did we explain to our children that as Christians we must live differently. Instead, we may have talked of financial costs, the dangers and risks, the illegality or ethics of certain behaviors. Did we tell them that specific directions for how we're to live are given to us in the Bible?

*"Teach me knowledge and good judgment,
for I believe in your commands."*
Psalms 119:66 (NIV)

We now see young parents who seldom express their faith at home, nor do they attend church. Learning about God and Christianity by osmosis through years of attending Sunday school and church services is certainly not the best mode; however, it provides more than if children never see the inside of a church, sit through a worship service, nor have at their disposal the age-level Sunday school materials available in most churches. Is it time for us to make up for this neglect, regardless of how incapable we may presently feel?

Most grandparents are willing to sacrifice time and effort for their grandchildren. We've seen this in many forms in the last three decades. Today the number of children who are being brought up by grandparents is a staggering multimillion. If there are grandparents who are now giving so much to their grandchildren by assuming complete financial and other responsibilities for them, can't all others agree to introduce, teach, and share our Christian faith with our grandchildren?

". . . because to this you were called so that
you may inherit a blessing."
1 Peter 3:9 (NIV)

We Can Do It! God's Help Is With Us

"Lord, you have been our dwelling place
throughout all generations."
Psalm 90:1 (NIV)

It's never too late to make a difference. Let's teach our grandchildren what our faith means to us today. We'll work to portray our religious faith in all we do, for in all our actions and words we have opportunities to reveal God's spirit in us.

In our plans for sharing our faith,
our actions are the most important piece of our plan.

Our grandchildren have little experience in connecting their world to Christian faith. We'll help them recognize and experience a life of faith in their world. All we do must be related to their contemporary world, for we cannot go back to the way it was when we grew up; and, they may not be able to move ahead into faith by themselves.

"Life can only be understood backwards
but it must be lived forward."
Soren Kierkegaard (1813-1855)

Let's use this opportunity to influence our grandchildren now. Don't despair, thinking it's too late and that you've really messed up. You haven't! After we've thought about what we can do and made our plans, we'll move forward and rejoice.

"You must do the thing you think
you cannot do."
Eleanor Roosevelt (1884-1962)

Pray often throughout the day, seeking God's available aid. To stay on track, we may need to renew our vow to share our faith with our grandchildren every day until it's as natural to us as breathing.

Each of our grandchildren is different in his or her own way, a very special child. For those with older grandchildren, we may feel it would be easier to share with younger children, or if they're very young we may wish to wait until they're older. This is called "looking for excuses." The ages of our grandchildren right now is exactly the perfect age for them to receive our beginning lessons in faith.

For those whose grandchildren are preschoolers, our impact can be unprecedented. Repetition is usually helpful to those in this age group, so be prepared to repeat the sections that capture their attention.

If our grandchildren are adolescents, our work may be more difficult, yet greatly rewarding. We may find they have many specific questions and they're eager to talk with us about our faith and living a religious life. Or they may resist our efforts to engage in discussions about faith, religion, or the Bible, and it will take much thought and preparation to dissolve their resistance. In these times, perhaps our best effort may be to speak honestly and tell them about our difficulty in putting faith into words and that we hope through discussing it with them, we'll find it easier to be open in all things from now on, especially with them. Letting them know we're striving to grow spiritually ourselves indicates that Christians never stop learning and growing in their faith.

Our grandchildren will quickly help us realize
that even though we may teach them what we know,
it's what we do that they'll duplicate.

As we continue toward success with our grandchildren, we'll continue reading our Bibles, praying earnestly to God about them and their parents, and about all children in our country who need a grandparent's concern. Having God's guidance is what sharing our faith is about, so let's never forget to acknowledge His presence, give thanks for His constant blessings, grace, and mercy, and stay on His path.

When you begin your involvement with your grandchildren, include the adults of your families by sharing your plans with their parents, always keeping them informed. The activities at the end of each chapter will assist you in this.

"Create in me a pure heart, O God, and renew a steadfast spirit within me."
Psalms 51:10 (NIV)

"You must make every effort to support your faith with goodness, and goodness with knowledge."
2 Peter 1:5 (NRSV)

Using This Book As a Guide

There's no intent in this book to change, nor to interpret or influence, anyone's theology, doctrine, belief, or church preference; instead it's meant to encourage and aid adults and entire families to grow together in their faith. It's written to stimulate our thinking as we evaluate and redefine our secular lives so our teaching of God and our Christian faith may be honestly expressed by us within the context of our own church's teachings and each family's religious heritage.

We don't need to be fluently acquainted with the Bible to share our faith with our grandchildren, nor must we be able to repeat specific doctrines, dogma, or liturgy. Instead, we may approach this experience as sacred work, using the manner in which Jesus looked upon children as our example. Our beliefs, sense of reverence, and our attitudes about our faith may be transferred to them through face-to-face conversations, through our actions at all times, and by using this book and its end-of-chapter activities.

Read the Table of Contents now to learn what is available so you may plan how you'll use each section. Use the book as a guide for adults who want to share their faith with children. Move about in it to satisfy your timing and specific interests, as well as to match the content to your grandchildren's ages. Select the activities you are most comfortable with at first, then return to the others later.

As we work with each separate chapter, reading through it before we develop our plan to involve our grandchildren will be beneficial. Doing this will bring buried knowledge to the surface, providing us with more to give our grandchildren.

We'll need a Bible readily available, and a Bible dictionary and a concordance will be helpful as you advance. Paperback editions are available in all the resources you may need. Use them often, mark them to increase their helpfulness, and show your school-age grandchildren how to use them. Look up Biblical references related to daily behavior, life's situations, your grandchildren's questions, and miracles which are part of your daily lives as a regular part of your plan.

Our job will be to
incorporate the Bible into their daily lives,
helping them discover
it is a contemporary guide for Christian living.

Be aware from the beginning that efforts to push religion and the Bible on our grandchildren in an unwelcome manner may provoke a backlash which may be difficult to overcome. Spouting words of faith while wielding the Bible over their heads will produce negative reactions. Let's practice intelligent restraint in our urgency. Instead, it's likely that as we think about how our faith relates to our every action during the day, our own interests will be heightened and we'll thirst for knowledge, and the wisdom to use it, while developing our experiences with our grandchildren.

If we hope
to do more for others,
we must first become more ourselves.

Our plans for melding our religious faith with our grandchild's life will be designed by each of us through our use of this book and other materials, by using the Bible and other resources, through our prayers, by talking with ministers, and through God's love and assistance.

May God bless you immeasurably
and guide you step-by-step
from the beginning of your endeavor
to share your faith with your grandchildren
throughout the weeks and months ahead.

FAITH

"Now faith is being sure of what we hope for and certain of what we do not see."

Hebrews 11:1

"Faith makes us, not we it."

Ralph Waldo Emerson

FAITH

Living By Faith

". . . the righteousness of God is revealed
through faith for faith: as it is written,
'The one who is righteous will live by faith.'"
Romans 1:17 (NRSV)

When we think of faith, our minds are on God, Jesus, the Bible, worship and the church, and doing God's will. Our faith is all these - all of them flowing to, from, and through faith. It is through God's presence in our lives and the universe, Jesus's life and ministry, the Holy Scriptures, worship, and service that faith abounds in our lives. We try to live faithfully and we've spoken of faith in our religious lives always, but how shall we explain faith to our grandchildren?

In the Gospels we read Jesus's references to faith,
"Your faith has made you well . . . Your faith has healed you;
Go in peace and be free from your suffering.
Take courage, don't be afraid . . . If you have faith and do not doubt
. . . If you have faith as small as a mustard seed."

In Matthew Jesus tells the disciples,
"I tell you the truth. If you have faith without any doubt
you can say to a mountain, 'Go throw yourself into the sea,'
and it will be done. If you truly believe,
you will receive whatever you ask for in prayer."

It may seem to us that Faith and Jesus are almost synonymous. Faith was a function of all Jesus' actions, his miracles, his teaching, and his life.

The Old Testament prophets spoke frequently of faith, proclaiming the requirement for proper faith in the lives of those who knew God. The lesser known prophet Habakkuk was puzzled by God's lack of response regarding Judah's wickedness, and more so about God's plan to turn Judah back to Him by using the barbarous Babylonians. He questioned God about the distress enacted upon the Israelites by the Babylonian king Nebuchadnezzar. God answered that the Babylonians would punish Judah for her wrongdoing, and added this judgment about the warring ruler:

"See, [Babylonia] is puffed up; their desires are not upright—
but the righteous will live by his faith."

Through his strong faith, Habakkuk accepted God's will. His prayer of trust and joy in chapter three expresses his awe and trust in God and His power, and his acceptance of all that God decrees.

Isaiah, Jeremiah, and other major prophets exemplified faith in their daily lives, expressing it in their writings as if it were a physical characteristic of their personhood.

The Book of Psalms is filled with verses in which faith is a prominent theme. Psalm 89 is a mournful plea prayed by David in which he recognizes God's faithfulness, though the King's dynasty lies in ruins. Faith or faithfulness is mentioned ten times in this Psalm, beginning with the first verse:

"I will sing
of the Lord's great love forever;
with my mouth I will make your faithfulness known
through all generations."

The most frequently remembered Old Testament example of faith is Abraham's extreme trust in God as he prepared to give up his son Isaac as God directed. His willingness to believe and to obey God without having any prior knowledge of where he was going nor what the outcome would be epitomized faith for Abraham's descendants as they struggled to be faithful people.

Though faith is the theme throughout the Bible, the language of faith is not easily conveyed. Helping our grandchildren understand it will be a great achievement as they translate the word "faith" into a life of faith. Our use of words and stories which they may easily interpret will be essential to successful sharing, while the practice of our faith in their presence day after day will reveal its true meaning.

Faith Is More Than Its Definition

"By faith Moses' parents hid him for three months
after he was born,
because they saw he was no ordinary child."
"By faith the people passed through the Red Sea
as on dry land."
Hebrews 11:23,29 (NIV)

Though we read the word "faith" often in the Bible, and we use the word in our religious practice, faith as a concept is not easily defined by us. It's more than its dictionary definitions of belief, conviction, trust, confidence, credence, and other words we find in our search for clarification.

The faith we read about in the Bible is a noun, yet it expresses action, power, motion, perseverance—all in a manner of energy being exerted. The above verses from the book of Hebrews express change and action through a life of exerting and bearing all in faith. They are from a significant passage, Chapter 11, which reminds the first century Christians about the strong faith of the Hebrews as they struggled to live as people of faith. Perhaps if "faith" were a verb in English as it was in Greek when it was written in the original New Testament scripture, we could more adequately define it by using action words.

We feel faith in our hearts,
we experience its action and power in our lives;
however, we find our words of definition insufficient
for such a profound spiritual concept.

Putting definitive meaning to faith has been difficult through many centuries for theologians and other religious peoples. We've seen this in differences between translations and revisions of the Bible through the years. One example: Ephesians 3:17, Revised Standard Version of the Holy Bible (1953), tells us we can know God through Christ and that *Christ may dwell in your hearts through faith.*

The Living Bible (1973) revised this passage and stated *Christ will be more and more at home in your hearts, living within you as you trust in him.* In this passage the word "faith" was avoided.

Martin Buber, (1878-1965) Jewish theologian, wrote of faith and the mystery of life: *Real faith means holding ourselves open to the unconditional mystery which we encounter in every sphere of our life which cannot be compressed in any formula.*[1]

Robert Fulghum, contemporary philosopher and author, wrote *Faith is a determination to keep in touch with the unnameable Being that dwells in the heart of all existence.* [2]

Anglo-American poet W.H. Auden (1907-73) gave us: *To choose what is difficult all one's days as if it were easy, that's faith.*[3]

Indeed, it's not easy to define faith.

Faith has been defined by theologians and writers in terms that leave us wondering what the words of the definitions mean. The following definitions are from a biblical dictionary for teens: *Faith has its ground in some being or power,* and *God's grace is the focus of faith.* Will our adolescent grandchildren clearly understand what these words mean? They won't, and neither will many church-going adults. These definitions are composed of religious-sounding words and concepts which also need defining.

We take faith beyond the religious into our secular world. It's present in our lives at all times, relevant to all minutes of our days, and experienced serenely—yet compellingly—by us. It is in this faith that we close our eyes to sleep at night.

"I am the Lord, I have called you in righteousness.
I have taken you by the hand and kept you."
Isaiah 42:6

Communicating Our Faith

"Consequently, faith comes from hearing the message and the message is heard through the word . . ."
Romans 10:17 (NIV)

We grandparents are people of faith, whether we've definitively studied faith or not. Tolstoy described faith as *one of the forces by which men live;* William James wrote *the absence of faith equals collapse*. These words tell us that faith is inherent in the living human heart. Our faith is *the* great legacy of our lives, a legacy which we instinctively yearn to pass on to our grandchildren. We'll begin to fulfill this yearning when we introduce our faith to them; or if we've done so already, we'll plan for specific discussions or events with them.

Faith is neither clearly defined nor explained through the use of religious-sounding words. We may accept obscure terminology from others, or even use it ourselves. However, children's comprehension of strange words involves their disposition at the time, the tone in which the words are spoken, and their ability to sort through thousands of sound bites passed into their minds by television every day. The secular world around them is visual, noisy, and not profound and their adjustment to our new words will perhaps take time and effort from all of us.

Let's think how our words will be perceived by young children and avoid wrapping our messages in mysterious language.

We've all heard children's transpositions. When our son was age three he often transposed our words into meanings which had more reality for him. Once his friend Reid came with his mother for a short visit just before nap time. Our son awoke remembering his visitor. "Where's Story?" he wanted to know.

Little ones endure with unusual skill in a world where language is mostly cryptic to them. One four-year-old demonstrated her adeptness through music. She loved the songs of Christmas and sang her favorite "Round John Virgin" robustly, clearly pronouncing her words. What does "yon" mean to a four-year-old; what does it sound like? To her, "virgin" was okay for John's surname—and, yes, some of us are round.

We may camouflage our faith by using words or concepts which we can't fully explain to our grandchildren; nor can they understand these mysterious words. They may smile, repeat precisely what we've said, yet not have a clue what the words mean. Perhaps, we may talk too rapidly and hurry past statements which need explanation. Or, are we repeating our message about faith as we heard it when we were children and we hadn't a clue about the meaning?

Instead of studying and talking with a minister or Bible teacher, we often ignore our own lack of knowledge. If we can't understand it, do we know if we should believe it?

Our lack of study may erode our faith, for without studying, reading the Bible, and praying for enlightenment, we may be faith-illiterate.

Though we may feel we adequately understand our faith and the meaning of Christian concepts because of our long history of going to Sunday school and church, engaging in continued thought, study, and prayer may assist each of us in providing Christian education to our grandchildren. Let's commit ourselves to thought, study, and prayer.

Many of us feel comfortable in our knowledge of our faith, yet we often deem ourselves inadequate to speak articulately about it—even though we feel God's nearness constantly, pray regularly, obey His commandments, and have remained faithful to Him throughout most of our lives. We may decline to pronounce aloud our heartfelt feelings about our faith, to pray aloud before others, or to introduce our faith to acquaintances who are hurting and needy.

One or two of the above statements may be true for some of us, all of it true for some, and none of it for others. Our stance in our own faith does not negate the possibility for any of us to share our faith with our grandchildren. Though we cannot verbalize what we know about God, or if our theology is a bit shaky, we still know how much our faith means to us and we want our grandchildren to share in it with us. Through the Bible's words we understand the confident reliance the Hebrews felt in God, and strive to make this our own faith.

"For where your treasure is,
there your heart will be also."
Matthew 6:21 (NIV)

Having presented the preceding questions and nudges regarding our faith in an effort to challenge thought and study, it's time now to reassure all grandparents that we are amply fitted to do this work. Our faith is strong, its foundation cemented firmly to the truths of historical Christianity as given in the Scripture and lived by us for years past. Our work with our grandchildren will be blessings to them and their parents, to our society and our nation. The manner in which we share with them will be our personal one, individualized and originating from love for them and for God, concern for their futures, and our answer to God's call.

When our grandchildren observe our interest in studying and reading our Bibles, when we pray with them and for them, when we mention God's word in our daily conversations with them, we will have already moved miles along His path, taking our grandchildren with us.

Continuing to Grow in Faith

"So the word of God spread. . ."
Acts 6:7 (NIV)

Our plans are made; we're looking forward to new experiences with our grandchildren. Then just when we're to begin, fear may overcome us and we'll use many excuses to delay the beginning moment of sharing. Fear is the dwelling place for many of us in too many parts of our lives. We're afraid of failure and the possibility of rejection, but through our determination and commitment, we won't permit this to hinder us in giving our greatest legacy to our grandchildren. Questioning our abilities at this point is acting as if God won't guide us all the way. A deeper knowledge of God comes to us through His existence in our unconscious minds and His support of our unrecognized abilities. This is His miraculous gift to each of us.

"For God is at work within you,
helping you to want to obey him,
and then helping you do what he wants."
Philippians 2:13 (The Living Bible)

Through faith we receive from God's inexhaustible resources the ability to go forward in sharing with our grandchildren. We may rely on Him for wisdom, love, compassion, strength, endurance—all the tools to carry out the work of sharing.

Faith has been discussed here not to provide rote answers, but to stir our thoughts and lead us to question, think, read more, pray more, and seek knowledge and wisdom regarding the Bible and Christianity. For humans, knowing all is not possible, neither is it possible to understand all we know.

Regularly reading the Bible helps us learn about faith. In the New Testament, the Letter to the Hebrews defines faith as *being sure of what we hope for and certain of what we do not see*. This book, Hebrews, lists many events in which the ancient Hebrews obeyed God as they were guided by Him through many centuries. None of their actions were easy, nor were the events ones which they themselves would have planned.

"It is God, for his own loving purpose,
who puts both the will and the action into you."
Philippians 2:13 (The Jesusalem Bible)

Faith is our link to God—a divine link—provided by Him. Our responsibility is to recognize this link. It isn't easily identified; we must seek it out; it's grounded in Him, not in ourselves, our worth, abilities, nor our service.

We may look at faith as our road,
or a journey
on a spiritual path.

Your grandchildren may become aware of how similar their quest in faith is to a journey, path, or road. This is an often occurring biblical phenomenon. The early Old Testament Hebrews wandered for forty years on the Way-to-the-Promised-Land; years later Jesus traveled the Road-to-Jerusalem where he knew trouble and danger awaited him; Paul's future was changed by the spiritual revelations he experienced while on the Road-to-Damascus; early Christian leaders were On-the-Road all over the known world of their day, developing churches; and today's missionaries Travel-the-Globe spreading God's word. Faith intends us to be disciplined, courageous, persevering, active and moving. It will hold us on a straight path.

There are two faces to faith: we have faith *in* God and show it by believing in Him and trusting Him, and by doing what He commands as we listen for his messages. Then there is the faith *of* God as described in the Bible—characteristics of God. He is always the same, dependable in all things, forgiving, delivering us through the sorrows in our lives, and guiding us on the path He shows us.

He is with us, helping us grow,
whether we acknowledge Him or not.

Faith is not a onetime experience. It builds up, we let it weaken, then it may become stronger, and then stronger still; yet it is at risk of weakening at any time. It's possible that we may live totally without recognizing faith for a period of time; and if we do, our faith may still be there—we're just not paying attention to it.

Faith is not a position we strive for and reach, and then we're set for life. It's a work in progress between us and God, as we live with assurance that God knows more about our lives than we'll ever know, and that He'll get us through them.

Our faith helps us cope
with our human existence.

Having faith doesn't mean we never have questions, or doubt; as we grow spiritually, we sometimes waver because our lives too often appear to be unstable. We see good people around us suffer illnesses and die young. Many who are good and not so good, young and old, are left destitute in the wake of storms all over the world, and plane crashes kill those on board, both Godly ones and unfaithful ones. We wonder about our faith and are sometimes overcome by anxiety. Will these events happen to us—and when they do, will we still trust God?

Faith also allows us to make mistakes. To have faith and have it impact our lives requires that we're willing to sacrifice some things at some times, that we act responsibly by doing what is required to have faith, and that we live lives of optimism most often, even in the face of adversity and arbitrariness. When we feel we're responding in faith to God, still we may feel insecure in our actions, and we may fail at times and make grave mistakes at other times because our faith is affected by the power of our minds—which may be questioning, insincere, halfhearted, and without confidence. However, the emotions of our hearts and our love of God also affect our faith, and God forgives our failures and our mistakes and continues to guide us on the path of spiritual growth.

Turning Our Grandchildren On to Faith

"She speaks with wisdom, and
faithful instruction is on her tongue."
Proverbs 31:26 (NIV)

We'll help our grandchildren grasp the meaning of faith and develop their involvement in a Christian life more easily if we use words and terms they understand. We'll avoid pressure, strictness, and never insist they learn exactly what we're talking about; however, we must not be so vague that their interest never catches on. We'll demonstrate our faith through our actions as we go about our lives, week after week. Our approach will be one that is appropriate for our grandchild's age level, in which we are honest and open in all we say and do.

Perhaps an ongoing study of our genealogy may enhance our grandchildren's understanding of faith. How did our immigrant ancestors come to this country more than two hundred years ago? Was it with broken hearts they left behind family members who were dear to them, most likely never to see them again? They sailed on ships unlikely to make the journey, leaving their property and material goods behind. Their belief in their need for religious freedom and their right to worship God as they desired provided them the courage to sacrifice in ways we cannot imagine. Their faith guided them through unseen territories and unimaginable circumstances.

In their adopted new land they acted responsibly in building new lives; and they found their faith in God and their previous beliefs about faith, hope, and love provided them with enough optimism to get them through their direst moments. Their faith helped them face troubles with the same attitude with which they acknowledged successes, always recognizing and thanking God.

We may compare our ancestors' immigration and their new lives to the time of the early church in the book of Acts. The new Christians were persecuted and denounced. They had to trust in God as they struggled to live where their lives were in danger at all times.

We want faith
to provide our grandchildren assurance
that they will live out all parts of their lives
with God's help,
and subsequent reassurance that all is well around them,
even in the darkest hours, because of Him.
We want, through faith, peace in their living
and meaning in their lives.
We want faith to be the pillar of their existence.

The following chapters will guide you in talking with your grandchildren about God, Jesus, The Bible, Worship and Church, and Living Our Faith in the World. Activities at the ends of the chapters provide projects for adults and children to stimulate interest and expand understanding. Through participation, you'll find the meaning of faith becoming clearer as you proceed.

You're encouraged to continue refining your thoughts about faith and how your life represents your faith to your grandchildren. Regardless of what we plan to do or say, it's the living we do that influences others most. This book's intent is that we love, pray, and live our faith in front of and with our grandchildren as we seek God's guidance in all we do.

GOD

Chapter One

It is written:
"Worship the Lord your God
and serve Him only."

Luke 4: 8 (NIV)

"Trust in him, and he will help you;
make your ways straight,
and hope in him."

Sirach 2:6 (The New Oxford Bible with Apocrypha)
(NRSV)

Chapter One

GOD

"No one has ever seen God; but if we love one another,
God lives in us
and his love is made complete in us."
I John 4:12 (NIV)

"Acknowledge and take to heart this day
that the Lord is God in heaven above and on earth below.
There is no other."
Deuteronomy 4:39 (NIV)

Telling others about God should be the most fulfilling events of our lives. Now a momentous opportunity lies before us. Let's share our faith with our grandchildren so they'll know God's blessings are available to them through relationship with Him.

Preparing Ourselves

Our first step is to decide what we want for our grandchildren. Which of our beliefs are dearest to us; which ones have provided us with life's deepest meaning? As we begin we may need resource materials to assist in clarifying or simplifying our thoughts. A visit to our public library or a book store, or a talk with a minister about our faith and about our project with our grandchildren, may help get us started; however, well prepared or not, we will never have to do this alone.

There is much help available to us. God hears every prayer and will help us share our faith. He reveals himself to us through the Scriptures, through Jesus, through His creation and others all around us.

Be prepared for young children's questions regarding God's appearance, God's location, God's magic, God's age, and the myriad of questions we'll surely be asked if we've stirred their interests.

God is physically invisible to us, so how do we explain that which cannot be seen?

If God can do all we say He can do, then He must be a magician. Put yourself in your grandchild's place as he ponders your words. If children have had little or no religious education, to whom will they compare God? Most young children will envision God as a powerful person much like their parents.

Stop, think about their questions, and ask God's guidance before you rush to answer them.

We talk about feeling God inside us as a way of describing who He is. Will our young preschool grandchild capture the true meaning of this explanation in a way that benefits and enables him to continue building on what we've told him? Or, will he lift his shirt and pat his tummy, asking if God is in there? These questions are serious to our grandchildren and are asked out of their childish experience and their minimal maturity. Let's think deeply about how we'll describe our religious feelings to children. And always, we must resist the temptation to dwell on their questions because they're cute, or to repeat them to other adults in their presence.

Portraying God as a human being limits everything about Him.

People, things, and events are earthly; God is unearthly and mysterious. Romano Guardini tells us that God's mysteriousness and His holiness makes us uncomfortable.[1] We may relate at first to this self-conscious or anxious inner feeling as we begin sharing with our grandchildren, but to help them capture the Greatness of God, it may be helpful to them in the future if we stretch our thinking to envision God not as man, but as being so vastly different from us that our minds must move in new channels. We will find our grandchildren are more adept at imagining unknown beings and concepts than are we who look for proof of everything in physical terms.

Human language is limited to describing only what we're capable of understanding. Our language can't fully describe God.

There are no limits regarding God, thus everything about Him expands: His Power, His Love, His Caring, His Creating, and His Eternity. By expanding our previous images of God and His Magnificence we draw near to the Mystery of God's Being so that we are encompassed in His Light, which brings understanding to us. Helping our grandchildren think of God expansively provides greater awareness for them as they fathom the forever expanding, profoundly loving potency that is God.

"How then can they call on the one
they have not believed in? And
how can they believe in the one of whom
they have not heard?"
Romans 10:14 (NIV)

Let's make our words informative and relevant to our contemporary world. If we're unprepared to answer when our grandchildren ask specific questions, perhaps replying, "I'm not certain. I'm still searching for answers," may be appropriate at the time. That keeps us where they know us and not in some unfamiliar land speaking a strange language of religious words. "Let's work together to see how many answers we can find" portrays to our grandchildren the reality that a Christian life is one in which study, prayer, and searching the Bible for answers continues throughout our lives.

God Is an All-inclusive Presence, Supporting All Existence

We know God through our relationship with Him. Now we'll work diligently to help our grandchildren develop their own strong and devoted relationship with Him.

"I want you to be happy,
always happy in the Lord."
Philippians 4:4 (The Jerusalem Bible)

Our Grandchildren's World Is Different From Ours

" . . . He has set eternity in the hearts of men;
yet they cannot fathom what God has done
from beginning to end."
Ecclesiastes 3:11 (NIV)

We don't have to understand God's plan to trust in His guidance and care for us. As we think of the differences between the environment in which we lived as children and that of our grandchildren, we realize how unalike they are, but we also realize that God is and was present and active in all these years. The changes in today's morals, standards, expectations—everything relating to family life—are different from the way we grew up. This doesn't mean that all our times were better, nor that all these times are worse.

The technological age has given us material advancement and provides us time to use in recreation and for ourselves instead of our always being on the job earning a living. Let's remain cognizant of these differences and our grandchildren's present environment. In this environment they have seen and heard almost everything through television's portrayals instead of through the story telling of times past. The individualization of family information has been lost, while the mass market of secular information abounds.

Their observation of the world around them and their television-pretend-world are combined to create their daily reality.

When we add the mystery of God to their unrealistic world they may quickly accept it, then just as quickly dismiss it as they dismiss some television portrayals—often remembering only the most inappropriate or scariest.

Very young children are often captivated by what they see, and they affirm the object's reality for the present time. Thus Minnie Mouse at Disney World can become their very best friend for a few days following a visit to the theme park. We must realize how secular input may impact their outlook for short periods of time as we begin to work with them.

[They] have mouths, but never speak,
eyes, but never see,
ears, but never hear,
noses, but never smell.
Psalm 115:5,6 (The Jerusalem Bible)

Young children use their senses to make sense of the world. In his own way, the three-year-old son of a minister friend announced that he needed more than language from the adults around him. He felt his nursery school teacher was somewhat too zealous about her students' hand washing, and after washing his hands for what he thought was simply too many times one day, he objected, "God and germs! That's all I ever hear, and I've never seen either one of them." Dirt and fingerpaint on his hands he understood; germs and God were't visible. Our language should be neither too abstract nor filled with nonsensible examples.

We need to be especially sensitive to their imaginative minds when we're telling stories from the Bible.

How quickly will our grandchildren change Biblical time to the present time in their minds? And how will they change God's developing relationship with the Hebrews into fearful images of a wrathful boogieman? We may have some difficulty adjusting to younger thinking, but we must never assume they are adjusting to grandparent thinking.

Many of us remember the story of Moses' experience with God in the burning bush. How many adults have told children this story in a way that leads children to see God as flaming fire? Speak carefully, especially when using examples that personify God. Every flame our grandchildren see does not depict God. Trying to portray God through physical manifestation usually fails, many times causing confusion or resistance—and sometimes, fear.

How can we bring the reality of God to playtime and all other good times and make our words meaningful and remembered by our grandchildren? Beyond that, how do we develop within them a yearning to learn more about God and add strength to their growing relationship with Him?

As we look for material to help us, we'll find that many reference volumes on religion have no listing for "God." Some refer to other listings, such as "Theology" or "Immanence." This indicates the rarity of words writers use to portray God, as well as the difficulty in doing so; and, it shows the reluctance we all have in being one who tells others what and who God is.

The Bible Tells Us About God

The Bible itself contains no definitions of God; however, there are many references to Him throughout the Scriptures which describe God's Being, His qualities and characteristics. John 4:24 tells us that God is Spirit, that He is without flesh, with no physical body. We learn that he is complete in wisdom, absolute in truth, infinite in power, has no bounds or limits, and extends beyond human comprehension. He is perfectly Holy and has revealed Himself to us through Jesus, through nature, and through many experiences with His people whom we find in the Scriptures.

In Deuteronomy 6:4 we learn there is only one true God. The Bible is not written to prove God's existence, but all references to God in the Scriptures assume the proof of God as self-evident for those who wrote the books of the Bible and for all who read it. God exists whether we believe in Him or not. He is the same regardless of how our minds or those of great spiritual leaders or teachers see him. He loves us whether we believe this or not, or whether we love Him or anyone, or not. Neither do we have to develop a certain degree of proficiency regarding our understanding of the concept of God. He is more different than we can possibly think of Him and greater in every way.

"You are worthy, our Lord and God,
to receive glory and honor and power."
Revelation 4:11 (NIV)

Telling Our Grandchildren about God Can Change Their Lives

"All thy children
shall be taught of the Lord."
Isaiah 54:13 (KJV)

It's a challenging task, this sharing of our faith that we're setting out to undertake; however, what we do now will positively impact our own lives and the lives of our families. This endeavor has consequences not just for our grandchildren, but also beneficial consequences for ourselves. It's impossible to do God's work without benefits accruing to us.

In a time when we're told regularly by scientists that life in all probability exists beyond our planet, we may use these concepts to help our grandchildren stretch their minds, their beliefs and understanding to include God's existence and his involvement in their lives. We can't see the planets, nor can we see God's Being; but to study either of them we must go beyond what we are physically able to see, open our minds and accept new knowledge.

"Nothing in all creation is hidden from God's sight."
Hebrews 4 :13 (NIV)

In Bill Moyers' *Genesis,* Professor Samuel Proctor reminds his distinguished colleagues that God was here long before the Bible. "If God is God, and God is Creator, we ought to learn something about God in the light of what we've learned about the cosmos and about the long drifts we see in history." He informs us we don't have to define God just as the ancient Hebrews did, that as we have personal experiences with God we learn more and more about Him as our lives go forward.[2]

We clearly understand the position we hold in our relationship with God through writer Catherine M. La Cugna's statement:

"One finds God because
one is already found by God."[3]
We'll never fail to find God when we seek Him.

As we begin our search for ways to tell our grandchildren about God, we'll look into our hearts for words and feelings to describe God. We feel the presence of the Divine, of God caring about us, leaving us with a sense of awe and wonder. Most likely our grandchildren have these special moments also, and they'll soon identify what we're describing. By revealing our deep personal feelings, we may describe to them what these feelings mean and how special they are.

Think of moments so full of wonder that in your stillness all you thought was "God!" Holding your newborn grandchild for the first time, looking at the most spectacular sunset you've ever seen, or a brilliant lightening bolt. And, of course, we have glorious feelings at the sight of a rainbow. Sometimes tears fill our eyes during movies when humanity's divine nature is sensitively portrayed. The tears of joy shed when we learn of a family member's safety after a frightening ordeal, the happiness of Thanksgiving family dinners with everyone present and healthy, and the gratitude for each morning that breaks with our lives intact and again being blessed, all cause responses of the heart rather than of the mind, bringing us to the knowledge of God.

". . . his lovingkindness begins afresh every day."
Lamentations 3:23 (The Living Bible)

Share with your grandchildren some precious memories which made you aware of God's reality and presence. I remember a very special sunset from many years ago. My husband and I were vacationing on the gulf coast of Florida and were driving lazily through a tiny village when suddenly we came upon a small group of people. They appeared to be engaged in a celebration. Curious, we parked and joined them. Very few were talking, then fewer and fewer were speaking, until quietness overtook us all as we stood transfixed looking out over the water. The sun was slowly sinking out of sight. Though no one said a word, I know most of us were thinking "God!" This was our first experience with what I learned is a daily celebration in many places along Florida's west coast.

We can explain God through His goodness and His blessings to us.

And, we can teach our grandchildren to show gratitude for everything in their lives—God's gifts and God's lessons. In our busy, materialistic world, we use our time and energy to work in order to earn so that we may buy; but nothing we buy can compare to the gifts God has given us freely. How do we compare a new dress or a video tape or a toy to sunshine, starlight, flowers, trees, birds, and air? Or to the love of a mother or father, brother or sister, which is given in the few moments we have together each day? Or to any simple joy?

In our prayers to God we often call Him Father. Children will relate to a parenting relationship, knowing the comfort of a parent's loving arms wrapped about them, easing their pains when they've fallen.

They can also grasp the love in God's promise that comfort is always available. The message of God's comfort is significant for our grandchildren because of their need for God's comfort and protection in this world where children are left alone, where adult fears are pushed onto youngsters, and where an explicit media is available twenty-four hours every day in every home. Our grandchildren will benefit greatly by simply knowing that God is available to them at all times in their scary world.

" 'For I know the plans I have for you,' declares the Lord,
'plans to prosper you and not to harm you,
plans to give you hope and a future.' "
Jeremiah 29:11 (NIV)

Another way to portray God's existence is through nature, comparing Him to the wind which cannot be seen, but which can be heard and felt through its energy and force. But in all our descriptive words and efforts to characterize Him, we will never get it exactly right. Who God is goes beyond our grandest conception of Him.

We have a long way to go to even imagine God, but we'll develop some answers because our imagination and thinking abilities are two of God's many gifts to us. Our work is to revere Him, love Him, feel His love, learn from His lessons, accept all we can ever know about Him, and continue always to search for greater knowledge and understanding of Him. Obedience to His love and to His will is required in our relationship with God. That is all we must do.

Romano Guardini in *The Art of Praying* assures us that God is never disappointed in us; He doesn't depend on our responses to Him. *He doesn't dwell in Olympian heights, indifferent to the plight of human existence. God loves us earnestly. He created us with the dignity of free will and responsibility.*[4]

Spiritual growth occurs one step at a time,
and by returning day after day to
the fundamental lessons of the Bible,
by spending time in prayer with God,
and by devoting periods of quiet time to listen to God's messages
we advance in our knowledge of Him.

Prayer and Quiet Helps Us Know God

"Ask, and It shall be given you."
Matthew 7:7

Prayer is our way of entering into conversation with God. It invites God's spirit into our lives. Its purpose is to bring us closer to God than we are when we don't pray.

David Jeremiah in *Prayer, The Great Adventure* claims prayer as his "Declaration of Dependence."[5] We recognize our dependence with humility and gratitude when we're fully settled into prayerful moments with God.

Dr. J.I. Packer recommends that we turn our knowledge about God into knowledge of God through meditation, then prayer and praise to God. Meditation, he says, is an *activity of calling to mind and thinking over, and dwelling on, applying to oneself, the various things one knows about the works and ways and purposes and promises of God.*

Packer calls meditation *an activity of holy thought, consciously performed in the presence of God, under the eye of God, by the help of God, as a means of communion with God.* [6]

Being quiet, still, expecting God to hear our prayers, feeling his presence in our hearts—this heals not just the body, mind and spirit, but our hearts as well. We have our past healed through God's forgiveness; our present filled with comfort and relief, the future assured through promise and hope. We feel as David did when he pronounced:

" I shall dwell in the house of the Lord.
Forever."

Before we end this chapter, let's include another word in our endeavor toward Christian understanding and developing a relationship with God. This word we'll keep in our hearts throughout our entire relationship with our grandchildren. The word is "soul."There's no physical proof by which to define soul: it's non-material, the immortal part of all of us; but that it truly is, is readily accepted by all of us. Seeking God earnestly and sincerely is to engage in remembering with the Spirit and bringing to our minds that which is already known by the soul.

If we think of our children's souls as their Being, we'll treat our grandchildren as God's favored ones. When we think of them as Douglas, or Jessica, without thinking of them as God's children, we tend to react to their behavior, their appearance, their possessions and styles of dress, their haircuts, and their language. When we relate to their souls, we connect to their Being, to God's presence in them. How can we then feel anything but reverence towards God for the gift of their lives when we're with them? And, when our relationship with them occurs in the Light of God, surely great miracles will take place in their lives and in ours.

". . . God is with you in everything you do."
Genesis 21:22b (NIV)

Chapter Activities

The activities following each chapter are intended to encourage growth and study through hands-on participation. Here is an opportunity to include everyone in the family to participate in learning more about your family's faith. Set aside times to talk about God, your beliefs and your Christian faith; also, include God in your everyday conversation and Christian concepts in your daily living.

Activities for all age groups are included through a combination of study, games, arts and crafts, field trips, and other projects. You may include additional activities which you feel your family will enjoy and which may lead to more conversation about your faith..

Before beginning any of the following activities, read through all of them. You may find you prefer a different order, or that you wish to eliminate one or two and substitute your own. Many of us will need to modify the activities in some manner because of the ages of our grandchildren. Include family members in every aspect of the activities as often as is feasible, from planning how you'll carry out each one to evaluating when you're finished and ready to move on.

"May the Lord continually bless you with heaven's blessings
as well as with human joys.
May you live to enjoy your grandchildren!"
Psalm 128: 5,6
(The Living Bible)

Activities for Chapter 1

Purpose

There are specific opportunities here for your grandchildren to experience God's love for mankind; to learn about God's creation; to see the magnificence of His plan for your family members, and all others of His universe; to feel His presence in the quietness of fields, woods, and sky; to understand His gifts of life and nature; and to develop a sense of genuine gratitude for all we've been given by God. By being closer to God through your sharing, God's will for you and your family may be unveiled for you, and the joy you share in working with your grandchildren will reflect your love of God.

1. Take a drive away from the city into the country. Find a place to get out of your car and spend time enjoying your surroundings. Look at the colors of the earth's floor. Think about the centuries of foliage and other natural materials that have fallen here and are continuing to create and change this specific spot of God's earth. Talk about the influence of the different seasons on the trees and the undergrowth beneath the trees and how they will be different in another season. Plan to come here again to see the changes.

Look for any animals or signs of God's creatures that may be living in the area, and think about how they prepare for change in seasons. Feel the air and the wind. Look at the sky. See how clouds move about, changing their formations. Discuss what impact the sky and clouds have on the earth.

Look for natural things on the ground: seeds, birds' nests, ant hills, rocks, sprouting plants, leaves, and insects. What is the smallest living thing you see? The largest? How are we connected to all of these? What did God mean when he declared creation to be "good"?

How may each of you express what you've seen of God's creation? Will you paint pictures, write a story or poem, take photos, or create a collage? Say a prayer of gratitude to God for his natural gifts and talk of God's continuing creation. He is never finished with the universe, with nature, or with His people. He is creating constantly and always, having nature renew itself day after day. We, as God's people, may also be renewed by God. Discuss the benefits of being renewed in our lives as you drive home.

2. Read what writers say about God and also about nature in books of quotations or poetry. Talk about any new ideas or words that are especially meaningful to you. Discuss what the writers may have been feeling when they wrote about God. Suggest that your school-age grandchildren start a notebook in which they'll write meaningful or helpful words they read. Many writers feel God speaks through them to their readers. Do you sometimes find messages in written material that speak clearly and profoundly to you?

3. Visit a church with your grandchildren to talk with a minister and perhaps an elderly church member about God's presence in their lives. Discuss what you learned about God from your conversations with these people? Do you think their understanding of God changed as they grew older and continued to worship God? What will you remember longest from their conversations? Talk with your grandchildren about the everyday dependence and connection which many people have with God and how this impacts their daily activities.

4. Borrow a church hymnal if you don't already have one of your own. Discover how many hymns about God are in the hymnal. Read aloud the verses of some of the hymns and discuss the beauty of the words. The words of many hymns existed long before they were put to music; some are words from the Book of Psalms and were sung by ancient Hebrews. Sing some of the hymns which are familiar to you. Work with your grandchild to write new words to a familiar hymn, then sing it to the familiar tune. Older children may write words about God and His creation to be sung to contemporary music. Encourage your grandchildren to use their creative abilities in all the activities you do, giving them freedom to select the approach they'll use. There is not just one way to do most things; all our God-given abilities are individualized within us, giving us opportunities to create.

5. Buy a CD or audio tape from the sacred music section in your music store. Listen to the music and the words about God. What are the vocalists saying? Is there anything in their musical message about God that is new to you? Talk about the message in the music. How many ways can you think of to learn more about God?

6. Discuss an appropriate statement to use as your family's "Motto of the Week." (Example: "I know God loves me," or "God really

is great," or "Always be thankful to God." Make computer posters or banners with the motto for your grandchildren's rooms. Put a smaller copy on the refrigerator door so you're reminded often. Choose a new family motto for each week, using your Bible and other resource materials, as well as your family's experiences.

7. Read the verses in Genesis about The Creation. Show your grandchild how easy it is to find *"In the beginning God created the heavens and the earth"* (Genesis 1:1, NIV). Plan an interpretation of God's creation and work on it together. This may be a drawing, painting, musical piece, drama, sculpture or mosaic, or dish garden. Talk about your own creative powers and help your grandchildren learn not only about creation, but how making proper plans and having characteristics such as persistency and patience in the work they do are parts of their being creative. Plan a visit to a museum.

8. Plan a visit to a plant nursery or garden center. Choose a tree to plant in your grandchild's yard. Talk about the kind of tree you'd like to purchase before you go. Do you want a fruit tree, a tree that will grow into a giant shade tree, a blooming tree, an evergreen? Discuss how much care the tree will need and how it should be appropriate for your region in order for it to thrive. Talk about the joy the tree will provide for your family as it grows bigger and bigger. Think about how long the tree will live, which is usually much longer than your grandchild will remain in his childhood home. If the family should move to another city, how will the tree be remembered many years in the future?

Plan a family outing to purchase the tree, bring it home, plant it in a special spot, then dedicate it to the family, and the family to it, in a special ceremony. Thank God for His creation of all trees.

9. Visit a large old church with stained glass windows. Ask the minister there or another responsible person to show you the windows and to point out the symbolism in them. Discuss how the windows and the church sanctuary reflect God to us.

10. Talk about what "God with us" means to us in our daily lives. Do we see God in our routine tasks and when we're with our friends as well as when we're alone? How can we remember He's always with us?

11. Encourage your grandchild to plan a quiet time every day in which he thinks about his family, his role in the family, about God's gifts to him and his family, how he might share with others who don't have as much as he has, and how majestic God's creation is. Help him develop a prayer time during this period.

If your grandchild is busy all the day every day, and his day begins with an alarm clock awakening him, you might suggest that the very first thing—while he's still in bed—he acknowledges God's presence in his life, thanks Him for this day, and asks for His care all the day long. For many children, once they're out of bed, there are many demands on them to hurry, to eat, to prepare to leave the house. Suggest they may discover their mornings will become happier and their days proceed more pleasantly when they've slowed down enough to say, "Thank you, God."

12. Grandparent, this one's for you. Pondering these lines will prepare you for some of the questions you'll receive from your grandchildren. Yes, these are childish questions, but they'll ask them because of their serious curiosity. You'll move along in your work with your grandchildren more productively if you have an answer ready for them. Read the questions, picture your grandchild asking them, and think of the meaningful, clear answers you'll give them. Trust in God and in yourself as you develop your thoughts.

a. What does God look like? Does He wear clothes?
b. Where is God? Does He live in churches?
c. How old is God? Will He die when he gets older?
d. How does God hear prayers if we don't say them aloud?
e. Does God like some people more than others?
f. When I'm bad, how will God punish me?
g. Can God make everything? Cars and airplanes?
i. Who knows most about God, ministers or grandparents?
j. If God can do miracles, why does He let bad things happen?
k. Grandpa was good; why did he die?

Have a good time with these activities and remember to relate them to the purpose for this chapter as you guide your grandchildren toward greater knowledge of God.

"Trust in the Lord with all your heart and
lean not on your own understanding;
in all your ways acknowledge him,
and he will make your paths straight."
Proverbs 3:5,6 (NIV)

Note

Our work in learning about God and seeking His presence in our daily lives is never finished, for we grow closer with each effort we make. Let's move forward with determination and *commit our endeavors to the Lord; trust in Him and He will make our work shine through our grandchildren for years to come."* (Pslam 37:5,6 paraphrased)

JESUS

Chapter Two

"Come to me,
all you who are weary and burdened,
and I will give you rest."

Matthew 11:28 (NIV)

"Don't you believe that
I am in the Father, and that the Father
is in me?"

John 14:10 (NIV)

Chapter Two

JESUS

"People were also bringing babies to Jesus to
have him touch them.
When the disciples saw this, they rebuked them.
But Jesus called the children to him and said,
'Let the little children come to me, and do not hinder them,
for the kingdom of God belongs to such as these.'"
Luke 18:15,16 (NIV)

Little children eagerly listen to stories about other children, and especially to those about babies. Most have heard about Baby Jesus through children's story books and nursery school dramas, for which they dressed as angels or shepherds at Christmas and sang "Away in a Manger". Many families display creches in their homes throughout the Christmas season and some place nativity portrayals on their lawns at Christmas—a stable, Mary and Joseph, a makeshift crib, and other figures to finish the story. These depictions of the Christmas story provide opportunities for us to explain the adult Jesus to our grandchildren.

Commercial businesses and other public properties remind us of the holiday through their displays, advertisements, Christmas music, and occasional inclusions of sacred music and references to the birth of Jesus. Television fills the weeks before Christmas with carols as part of their advertising, and sometimes there is a mention of Jesus' birthday. If at no other time in the year, at Christmas we find symbols of Christianity visible in our secular world; and a few more people attend church services to observe the pageantry. We grandparents should capture this opportunity to amplify the bit of information received by our grandchildren during the Christmas holiday. What they learn from their environment is helpful as a starting point, but this small fragment of knowledge should not be left as the only message our grandchildren have about Jesus. The bits and pieces about Jesus presented at Christmas can be the crack in the door that gives us entry to move in with the entire story and it's blessing for our grandchildren.

Let's magnify what they see and hear because most children haven't received an adequate portrayal of Jesus' life, his ministry and his teaching, and how this knowledge and witness can change their lives.

Let Your Faith Bear Fruit
Share the Miracle of Jesus with Your Grandchildren

"Continue in what you have learned and have
become convinced of,
because you know those from whom you have learned it,
and how from infancy you have known the holy Scriptures,
which are able to make you wise
through faith in Christ Jesus."
2 Timothy 3:14, 15 (NIV)

There was no Christmas celebration during Jesus' lifetime. Christmas as a religious holiday was established many years after his death as a way of recognizing Jesus, honoring his life, and remembering the greatest story ever told. Observation of this special historical event as a religious holiday is established today within the period of time that we've set aside to revere Jesus, denoting the great significance of his life here on earth.

We can keep our family's Christmas observance sacred and minimize the secular by attending church services available in our community; reading the stories of Jesus' birth from the Bible and children's Bible story books; by listening to recorded Christmas music, including *The Messiah; and* by taking gifts to shut-ins or needy children as Jesus portrayed to us. How we celebrate and honor this season will determine for our children whether Christmas is a secular holiday or a religious celebration.

There are many different ways we celebrate Christmas within our families and also within Christian churches. Candlelight services, special music, dramas, advent services at church and advent calendars at home—all provide opportunities to spend time in worship of God as we acknowledge Jesus' importance to us.

Whatever special celebrations our families adhere to,
and whatever our church's denomination
or its specific dogma directs for our observance
at Christmas,
to be Christian for all of us means that
we follow Christ's teachings
and his life's example throughout our lives.

We're to make the observance of Christmas a time to celebrate the good news of Jesus' birth, his life and message of selfless love, and goodwill to all people, and to emulate his relationship with God.

Throughout all the year, by following Jesus' teachings and by using the foundations of the faith we grandparents have, we are prepared to teach Christian concepts to our grandchildren. There will likely be many times we'll search for words which will have meanings clear enough for a four-year-old to grasp, or for a doubting adolescent whose budding scientific mind comprehends facts astutely and uses those facts to learn even more facts, quickly discarding any which can't be proven and giving it no place in his secular world.

The work ahead with our grandchildren may be extensive, and it will be progressive. Telling the Christian message requires that we move much further than staying with the baby in the manger and that we continue on our path throughout their childhood.

"Do not conform any longer to the pattern of this world,
but be transformed by the renewing of your mind."
Romans 12:2 (NIV)

Jesus and Christianity

"So from now on we regard no one
from a worldly point of view. Though we once
regarded Christ in this way, we do so no longer."
2 Corinthians 5:16 (NIV)

Christianity exists today because Jesus lived two thousand years ago and because of his crucifixion and resurrection. The Gospels tell of the activity of only fifty-two days of Jesus' adult life.[1] Yet, in these few days, the list of all that Jesus accomplished astounds us. Teaching, preaching, gathering disciples, selecting and training apostles, traveling on foot, performing miracles, settling disputes, healing, and changing lives—all this information and the transformation of life about him makes us feel we've read about many years of his life. These verses about the fifty-two days is what our faith is built on, what Christianity and the Christian church has as its foundation

The impact and duration of Christianity is truly unique. For two millennia people all over the world have been spiritually moved and their daily lives directed by the teachings of Jesus. Our lives this day would be very different had he not lived.

There is no religion in all the world that is more wide-spread than Christianity; nor is there one that has had such a profound influence on daily life, on believers and nonbelievers alike.

This ongoing, lasting influence and the personal grace we each have received through Jesus' life on earth is the influence and grace we desire for our grandchildren. He taught that God is divine, and is the Holy Spirit whose Being is felt by us through physical and mental experiences and through relationships. He taught that our Father is not a God of retribution but a God of forgiveness, that all people are God's children and therefore we're brothers, and that the key to a spiritual life is to provide loving service to individuals other than ourselves.

Jesus was focused on what God wanted him to do. In John 17 we find that Jesus didn't let even his overwhelming sense of anguish discourage him from carrying out God's will. In these last prayers he portrayed the way of life to which all of us should aspire—concern for others even in our most difficult moments.

We are given many spiritual challenges by Jesus.
Sharing our faith with our grandchildren is
a superb challenge for us,
one that is ongoing and may be demanding. It could require
sacrifice by us, and will require love and care.

Our personal faith and our basic religious beliefs were most likely passed to us by our families, with the help of various ministers and Sunday School teachers. Some of us may feel incapable at this point, having accepted throughout our lives information about Jesus, God, and our faith without much thought about our family's religious heritage and its practices. Our faith may be undeveloped in our own minds, leaving us with understandings which feel childish, shadowed, and unclear. In some ways, we all may find ourselves catching up on our faith as we work with our grandchildren.

Study for all of us will be enlightening and uplifting
as we renew our path of Christianity
and lead our grandchildren on it.
We will learn as they learn, growing together.

Once we make the decision to share our faith and have concern for our grandchildren's spiritual lives we will be empowered to great achievement in our quest. God is with us all, all the time. Acknowledging Him brings power and equality to us in everything, including our capability to understand Him. Jesus taught that we are to work on our spiritual growth throughout our lives. We are all to do this, the learned and the unlearned, the young and the old.

"Then Jesus told his disciples a parable to show them
that they should always pray and not give up."
Luke 18:1 (NIV)

Jesus' Life

"Come to me, all you who are weary and burdened, and I will give you rest."
Matthew 11:28 (NIV)

Jesus' background was very humble and he easily could have grown into adulthood and followed the trade of his earthly father. With the circumstances of his birth and childhood, without God's intervention it would be likely that today, two thousand years later, we would not know about him.

Jesus was born in Bethlehem near the end of the reign of Herod the Great (who died 4 BC). Some write that he was one of at least seven children, whose family lived in a small Jewish village known as Nazareth. By the age of five he presumably spent his days studying at his family's synagogue, as was the custom for young Jewish males. His education consisted primarily of thorough instruction in the Hebrew Scriptures and learning the old Israelite language so he could eventually read from the ancient passages of Isaiah and other prophets, the prayers and hymns of David, and Hebrew law. In his young adulthood he probably followed in his father Joseph's footsteps and worked as a carpenter. His entire time on earth was exceedingly brief in comparison to the length of our lives today.

Approximately 28 CE
Jesus was baptized in the River Jordan by a prophet known as John the Baptist.

John was Jesus' cousin and was most likely more well known than Jesus would become during his lifetime. The rite of baptism was not practiced by the Hebrews at that time as it wasn't a part of Jewish law. Baptism symbolized that one's old life was washed away and the person baptized was then new as an infant, cleansed of his sins. John the Baptist made this rite available to everyone, including those who were not allowed to receive the instruction of Judaism. Tax collectors, the poor, females, and many others were denied the opportunity to study the sacred scriptures and were excluded from participation in a full religious life. Now anyone who desired baptism and a connection to God could receive it through John the Baptist.

Jesus began his ministry soon after his baptism by teaching in synagogues,thus becoming known as rabbi and teacher. His teaching was revolutionary. Teaching about love was strikingly different from the teachings of the Scriptures in which the laws were magnified and the Psalms spoke of God's majesty and His rule over man. Jesus taught that people should love each other, their neighbors, and their enemies. He reminded them that God causes the rain to fall and the sun to shine on both the just and the unjust, treating all mankind with equality and giving us opportunities to choose actions which will bring either distress and havoc to our lives, or actions which will further reward us.

Jesus gave us the greatest commandment, telling us exactly what we're to do:

"Love the Lord your God with all your heart
and with all your soul and with all your mind
and with all your strength."
and
"Love your neighbor as yourself."
Mark 12:30,31 (NIV)

Some prophets in the region thought Jesus was the Messiah who had been expected for many years. We read about this expectation in Isaiah from the Old Testament. Jewish leaders, who were concerned that Jesus would cause people to question their authority, inflicted much pain and trouble upon Jesus, accusing him and making his daily life difficult and perilous. Jewish authorities called Jesus a rebel, threatening his life and denying that he was spiritually connected to God in any way.

During this time Jesus had no human person to lean on when troubles mounted. He could have given up and simply stopped teaching and meeting with people because of all the problems he had. He could have found another way to live and left the area, going where no one knew him. Instead, in his short time on earth he gave those who followed him joy, hope, counsel, encouragement, healing, and love directly and through his own life's examples.

Jesus became a wandering teacher and walked everywhere, moving about frequently to see more people. Travel was measured then by "an hour on foot;" few of us can relate to this as we are in and out of our cars which carry us each mile, and each hour.

Usually speaking Palestinian Aramaic, Jesus told parables about what he described as the Kingdom of God. These descriptive stories made his messages easily understood by everyone. Multitudes heard him, believed his message, found encouragement for their lives, and were healed by him. All wanted to hear more, and many followed him from town to town to hear him again and again.

When Jesus went into Jerusalem to teach, his enemies implemented their plan to trick him into incriminating himself. Jesus thought of himself as a prophet, but he called himself the Son of Man. This was not a title, instead it meant that he saw himself as human; however his enemies used these few words to cause great trouble for him.

"Every day he was teaching at the temple.
But the chief priests,,the teachers of the law and the leaders among the people were trying to [harm] him."
Luke 19:47 (NIV)

". . . and they plotted to arrest Jesus in some sly way."
Matthew 26:4 (NIV)

Jesus' Great Love for God

"Father, if you are willing, take this cup from me;
yet not my will, but yours be done."
Luke 22:42 (NIV)

Jesus loved God in a way no one had ever loved God. He lived his life with pure love for everyone and profound faith in God. He was able to teach all those around him more about God's relationship to man than they had ever known. He helped them understand God's love for all humanity and taught that all people should love God and each other. He personified love in all his words and actions.

The people who followed Jesus hadn't previously known God in the way Jesus taught. Instead, their concern was to follow Jewish law and to expect God's wrath and the punishments to be dealt them if they disobeyed the laws. The love Jesus taught was a new concept related to God. Jesus' teaching upset some of the people of the synagogues because they thought they already knew all about God, and this threatened their authority. They became jealous of Jesus and wanted him to go away, to disappear. It wasn't long before the enemies of Jesus had him killed. They had not learned the lessons of love.

Jesus' death was a grievous matter. But through some terrible events, blessings can occur.

Jesus was never to be forgotten.
Many who had known Jesus
remembered all that he'd taught and
they implemented these teachings into their daily living.
They prayed the way he'd taught them, and
many times they felt him close by even though
they knew his body was no longer with them.

For many years after Jesus' death his teachings continued to be passed on orally, with very few words written about Jesus' life on earth. Later, some of his followers began writing about him and his teachings and these works came to be known as our Christian Scriptures, which have in the past and continue today to inspire and influence the daily ethical and spiritual lives of millions of people around the globe. Several years after Jesus'death churches were established by followers of Jesus' teaching; but before the churches were founded, these people met in homes. These followers were first known as Believers, and later they were called Christians.

"So we must listen very carefully to the truths
we have heard,
or we may drift away from them."
Hebrews 2:1 (The Living Bible)

How Will Our Grandchildren Know Jesus?

Tell me the stories of Jesus I love to hear;
Things I would ask him to tell me
If he were here:
Scenes by the wayside, Tales of the sea,
Stories of Jesus, Tell them to me.

First let me hear how the children stood round his knee,
And I shall fancy his blessing
Resting on me;
Words full of kindness, Deeds full of grace,
All in the lovelight of Jesus' face.

These words were written by William H. Parker (1845-1929) and have been included in hymnals since Frederic A. Challinor set them to music in the last century. Read these words aloud to your grandchildren. Then sing them if you know the tune. Close your eyes and see your grandchildren with Jesus.

To make Jesus sound like a real person to our grandchildren, we may gather Bible story books, music, poetry, and art to help us find meaningful words like these of William H. Parker to share with them. Whatever we do, telling children about Jesus will be the foundation of sharing our Christian faith; and our knowledge of him may be transposed into blessings for our grandchildren.

Jesus, a humble, poor child, grew up to become known all over the world for more than two thousand years. He grew to adulthood reflecting God at all times, in all situations, and influencing everyone he met. His influence challenged the thoughts and behavior of people everywhere, and continues today to do so.

Jesus never traveled far from his birthplace. He loved his family, was good to his friends, and was always kind. His life was very different from our lives today. He had no telephone to call the disciples for meetings, no television to see the evening news nor for entertainment. He didn't speak English, but could read Hebrew. He never visited Disney Land, never ate pizza, never rode in a car. He never went to a mall, never had a bicycle or roller blades, never used a computer. He lived in the natural world around him, and his examples for living were stories of his world in the outdoors

The times of Jesus were very different from our times, but how he responded to God is a great example for us two thousand years later.

Jesus listened to God's directions and he let God lead him in all he spoke and did. He lived his life as he taught, being compassionate to those who were hurting; and as he believed, accepting death on the cross. He brought hope to those who followed him; he is the entire foundation of Christianity.

There was no world-wide system of communication during Jesus' life, nor during the following long ages when Christianity was being established. During his life, Jesus' entire circle of influence was limited to walking distance. The only people who knew him were those who personally saw and heard him. Discuss this with your grandchildren. How likely would it have been that knowledge of Jesus never reached far enough with enough importance to make this great impact on our lives two thousand years later? Is it God's will that the words of Jesus, stories of his deeds, and his teaching have been carried to every corner of the world by his followers throughout all the years since his death?

"Jesus said, 'Let the little children come to me,
and do not hinder them,
for the kingdom of heaven belongs to such as these.'"
Matthew 19:14 (NIV)

Jesus, The Foundation of The Church

"He will bring you a message through which
you and all your household will be saved."
Acts 11:14 (NIV)

Our grandchildren will know Jesus through our teaching and with the aid of the Sunday School teachers in the church they attend. There is little opportunity today for children to obtain this message outside of family and their church. Because of this, we may need to work diligently on our introduction of Jesus to our grandchildren.

Jesus reveals God to us through his humanity.
He is the God-bearer for all time.

As Christian churches spread, man's influence was felt in the theology which proliferated throughout the churches. Henry Ward Beecher (18113-1837) said of theology: *It's the science of [man's] mind applied to God.* In some instances over many years, Jesus' message of love and brotherhood became distorted. Different interpretations eventually altered Jesus' basic Christianity as dogma took over. Later these interpretations resulted in the existence of different churches and denominations.

Diversity can make Christianity fuller
as we accept and
study our differences
and learn the gifts and benefits of them.

Our faith grows stronger through study, thought, discussion,and prayer, knowledge comes to us through openness, not through closed minds. Also, is it possible that none of the different interpretations are absolutely perfect, and that all church leaders and church members work through the years to become better people and better churches through greater knowledge of Jesus and his message?

The differences in theological interpretations by scholars and churchmen are unimportant in Jesus' overall message of love for each other and love of God. Nor must we have great depth of understanding of Biblical scriptures as we first read them. What does matter is that the search for truth and spiritual experience by each individual should be awakened and sustained, and that Christ's message of love and spiritual growth should be kept active in our lives. Having spiritual awareness is more than taking part in rituals, sacrificing, and praying in public. Our spiritual life is an inner experience which we express outwardly through tolerance, acceptance, love, and service to others, and in the fellowship of Christians around us.

Jesus' message is based on faith, love, joy, peace, forgiveness, gentleness, and continued growth. It encourages harmony between persons, nature, and God. We can lead our grandchildren to go beyond and around dogma and theology by reading and studying their Bibles, praying often, and depending upon God for greater understanding of all they learn. Their daily growth through Christian experience will help them glean deeper meaning from Christ's teaching.

Jesus Calls Us

"Just as He who called you is holy,
so be holy in all you do."
1 Peter 1:15 (NIV)

The Christian person follows the teachings of Jesus and accepts the gift of his life through faith. He makes decisions based on an understanding of God's will for him. He has choices to make throughout his life and he is responsible for the decisions he makes. How can our grandchildren pattern their lives after the life of Jesus if all they know is the sweet childish story of Jesus and shepherds and wise men?

A Christian home maintains Jesus' spiritual quality in all its daily activities.

Family members acknowledge that they live in the presence of God. His presence isn't experienced just by ministers, priests, saints, and mystics. We don't need to remind ourselves we are Christians anymore than we need to remind ourselves we are Americans or that we are men and women. Our daily lives reflect the fact that we are God's people. Christian families are fair, they demonstrate a spirit of sharing, with each individual recognizing the rights and responsibilities of each other. Neither sorrow nor joy come to individual members of the family, but to the whole family, and there are no strings attached to the Christian love they share. Their continued spiritual growth is patterned as becoming—becoming Christians, becoming enlightened, becoming closer to God.

"To those who have been called,
who are loved by God the Fatherand kept by Jesus Christ:
Mercy, peace,and love be yours in abundance."
Jude 1:1 (NIV)

Living as Jesus taught us to live and guiding our grandchildren to follow his guidance is our goal. This may be difficult, but it is not impossible—even in today's world. Jesus' world was also wrought with severe sociological, economic, and political troubles. Around him at all times was danger, prejudice, poverty, illness and death, and problems we will never experience in our lives.

It is in times like these that Jesus' ministry is sorely needed. Our grandchildren may grow into adults who carry the banners that help change the world. God's promise is still with us, and each of us has a part in bringing about the reality of that promise. Let's help our grandchildren find their way on The Way, that they may mature into men and women who serve God in everything they do.

"[Good grandparents] bring good things out of
the good stored up in them."
Matthew 12:35 (NIV)

". . . The effective, fervent prayer of a righteous
man avails much."
James 5:16 (NKJV)

As you begin the following activities, read through all of them before planning a specific activity. Then arrange your participation with your grandchildren in ways that will be more meaningful with regard to their ages and their interests. There will be many experiences from your own faith which you'll want to include in this material about Jesus. Use words your grandchildren are able to understand with the greatest meaning for them.

Activities for Chapter 2

Purpose

Your grandchild's knowledge about Jesus, his life and ministry, and his influence on our world today may be enhanced by participating in activities such as these. We all learn more when we read, study, and practice, and spending time and thought on Jesus and his life will make us more knowledgeable as well as stir our desire to know more. Please use your love for God and Jesus to help you add to these activities and to change them so they become more meaningful to your grandchildren.

1. Use an up-to-date atlas or globe to locate Palestine. Look in an encyclopedia, a study Bible, or other resource material for articles about Palestine during biblical times. Take a trip together to the library to find several books in the religion section that will provide you with pictures of Jesus' geographical area during his life. Look at these pictures and maps and talk about daily life as it was at that time.

2. Help your grandchildren develop a sense of time so they realize what the span of two thousand years means. Begin by comparing your early childhood to your grandchild's daily experiences. For many of us, in our childhood there was no television, no computers, and fast food was a peanut butter sandwich. Think of the differences in the way you grew up and the way your grandchildren are growing up. Next, compare your grandchild's life to your parents' (his great-grandparents') childhood lives.

Continue this comparison back to the time of your family's immigration to our country, then further back to the invention of the printing press and the first books, and other early discoveries and inventions. During each step back, have your grandchildren close their eyes and imagine their lives in those years as you describe the conditions of life about them. Finally have them describe how they think

Jesus spent his school days. What did his books look like? Did he use ballpoint pens? Did he have a backpack for his books?

3. Begin a genealogy project with grandchildren who are ten and older. This project will be a work in progress for many years, but it can be personally fulfilling for everyone including members of your extended family. No time is better than now to begin. Computer genealogy programs will make it easy for you. If you're not familiar with computer programs, talk with members of your family who enjoy computer work and have them begin this project for you. Eventually, the entire family may find themselves engrossed with you and your grandchildren in this project.

A genealogy project teaches children that family life is to be cared for and cherished. They will recognize the importance and strength of the family, the sacrifices that were made for them in years before they were born, the struggles of those who lived and died without an opportunity to realize any success from their hardships, thus leaving the benefit to family members in later generations. Grandchildren will begin to care about the beliefs in the family as they discover how they were passed to them through many generations. They'll develop an understanding of shared responsibility and how it has made us who we are, that we're responsible for those who come after us, and that we're to be sincerely grateful to those who came before us. Discuss also how our religious beliefs are still the same as those of our ancestors and how Jesus carried forward the faith of Abraham, David, Isaiah, and others who followed God years before Jesus was born.

4. Choose one of Jesus' parables to read and talk about. Change it into a modern day version and plan to dramatize it during a family night together.

5. Find a video tape that portrays the story of Jesus as an adult. Watch it together and plan for one family member to identify times in the film when Jesus was kind, another to list the different teaching messages he gave, and still another to find him forgiving others.

Talk about each discovery after viewing the video and discuss how it is sometimes difficult to do as Jesus did, but how important it is to think about our behavior, our attitudes, and how we spend our time.

6. Read a Bible story at night before going to bed. Choose a story about Jesus and children, and one that is correct for your grandchildren's ages. Where there is more than one grandchild, you'll want to find a separate story for each one's specific age. Often the cause for failing to understand our faith is the result of hearing it discussed (or preached) in adult language and religious terminology. Children don't listen to that which they don't understand; instead they put it into a category of: "I don't want to hear it because it all sounds alike and I don't understand it." Our grandchildren will do as we did years ago.

7. Plan a full day of kindness to others and love for everyone. Have your grandchildren think about how they'll accomplish this the evening before. On arising they will be kind throughout the day. (If there are times they forget, your exemplary kindness in how you explain "back-sliding" will bring them back on course.) At the end of the day, talk about what they did and how they felt when they did it. How did it affect others? How did they feel when they slipped up and were unkind? What did they do about these times? Also, how do they feel now and is this something they can do every day?

8. Plan a meal using foods from Jesus' time. Pita and matzo bread will serve as the unleavened bread Jesus ate. Figs, grapes, dates, nuts, olives and olive oil, and goat cheese are good foods we eat today and which provided many meals in the time of Jesus. Your study together will reveal other foods from the area. Discuss how they would have prepared a meal, having no supermarkets, no paper napkins, no food processor, no electric range, no running water and other conveniences.

9. Jesus gave us a special prayer to God that has served Christians and others for many years. Learn the *Lord's Prayer* together—this prayer that has been spoken for two thousand years. Study the sentences, phrases, and the full meaning of its entirety. Suggest that your grandchildren use this prayer for their mealtime grace for a week. Let them know that adults often use this prayer when they are asked to pray before a group, and that people in many churches say this prayer together aloud every Sunday in their worship services. Millions of people over the entire world pray together *The Lord's Prayer* every Sunday, often standing together to indicate "We

stand before you, Lord." We're connected to each other as God's people by speaking this prayer.

10. Have your grandchildren imagine they are disciples of Jesus. Have them describe how they would feel to be told by Jesus today to "Go out and proclaim the good news. And cure the sick, raise them out of the beds in the hospitals to go home well, make the homeless people clean and give them jobs and hope, take negative and violent urges from people's hearts and tell them that God is near and loves them." Discuss how this might change their lives and how people may react to them. How would this kind of behavior by many people change the world?

Note

All your sharing about Jesus with your grandchildren should be within the beliefs and practices of your own church. Information aboutThe Lord's Supper, the crucifixion and resurrection, and other specifics which you may include will benefit your grandchildren beyond what has been provided here.

Participation in Communion services and other rituals are meaningful to young children when an adult who cares about them explains the procedures carefully. Plan to share these blessings with your grandchildren as you advance in your sharing.

THE BIBLE

Chapter Three

"All scripture is inspired by God and
can profitably be used for teaching,
for refuting error,
for guiding people's lives and
teaching them to be holy.
This is how the man who is
dedicated to God becomes fully equipped
and ready for any good work."

2 Timothy 3:16
(The Jerusalem Bible with Apocrypha)

Chapter Three

THE HOLY BIBLE

"So great is my veneration for the Bible that
the earlier my children begin to read it
the more confident will be my hope
that they will prove
useful citizens of their country
and respectable members of society."
John Quincy Adams (1767-1848)

"Whatever merit there is in anything that
I have written is simply due to the fact
that when I was a child my mother daily read me
a part of the Bible
and daily made me learn a part of it by heart."
John Ruskin (1819-1900)

"In the beginning was the Word, and the Word was with God,
and the Word was God."
John 1:1 (NIV)

The Bible is more than special words written on pages; it's God moving among us creating, revealing, renewing. Without the Bible we would not know God in all the ways we know Him today. It's extremely difficult to imagine what our lives would be if the Bible didn't exist. Think for a moment: see in your mind all the years of your life filled with your family, friends, and acquaintances, all the events of your life including the joyous and the unfortunate, your successes and your failures. Now try to think of these years existing and passing without a recorded word of God. We cannot begin to imagine this. We're dependent upon the Scriptures for knowledge of who God is and who we are, and for the guidelines by which we measure our lives.

We have the Bible not because of human endeavors and extensive research, but because of God's own revelation to human beings.

"The Bible is the only book in the world that when you read it, the Author shows up."
Anonymous

His Word doesn't exist in a vacuum; it's neither abstract nor unclear. His plan for us and the world has always been distinct. It was available to ancient peoples and later civilizations, before books as we know them existed. Its influence over all segments of human life was, and still is, powerful—causing changes and developments that turn lives around and inside out.

This chapter will enhance our current Biblical knowledge so we may bring the Bible to life for our grandchildren. Each of us reads the Bible to learn what it teaches about God and to receive God's messages. We're taught through the Bible's majestic symbols, metaphors, analogies, poetry, history, and narrative—all telling us about our place in God's plan.

Our goal now is to help our grandchildren become familiar with the Bible in their discovery of who they are as God's children and why they are here.

We'll help our grandchildren discover the constant relationship between God and Man, God and Nature, and Man and Man, and learn how God intended His people to live in His world; and, we'll introduce them to specific individuals in the Bible through whom God worked as He led His ancient people. The stories about these people in the Old Testament tell us who we are. We want our grandchildren to learn *what really matters* in their lives just as the people of the Bible learned about what mattered to them. In Genesis we listen to the conversations of the ancient people as they crossed the Red Sea. How could they do that! We discover our own potential is far greater than what we accept for ourselves.

Our grandchildren will learn about people throughout the world and the ages who've heeded God's messages found in the Bible. We'll study with them about the work of God's dedicated people who later were responsible for producing the written Word, who completed the difficult task of translating early Scriptures accurately so that we may read the Bible today written in our own language. Also, we'll think about the great influence the Bible has had upon art, literature, architecture, social norms, and other important aspects of daily life throughout history.

Learning to use and study the Bible with reverence, and to use indexes,concordances, commentaries, Bible dictionaries, and other resources available to guide us will add to our grandchildren's understanding.

As we do our Bible reading in preparation to work with our grandchildren, we'll remember how much of this great book we already know; then through our continued reading we'll gain even greater understanding.

When we read the Bible,
we're in communication with God.
We're also in touch with the ancient people
who believed in God,
who put all their faith in Him as they experienced
good times and bad times in their lives—
often forsaking God, then returning again to Him
from whom they received strength, refuge, hope, love,
blessings, guidance, forgiveness and unending care.

Read this entire chapter, including the activities, before you begin Bible study with your grandchildren. By doing this you'll be better prepared to answer questions and to help them handle and use the Bible. You'll also be ready to meet objections many adolescents automatically invent regarding Bible study.

In *Halley's Bible Handbook* George Muller tells us, *The vigor of our Spiritual Life will be in exact proportion to the place held by the Bible in our life and thoughts.*[1] Let's instill within our grandchildren a love and respect for God's Holy Word. Neglecting to do this may leave them to life-long struggle, hurt, and despair without knowing of God's presence and the comfort that's theirs by knowing Him.

"God's word is alive and working
and is sharper than a double-edged sword.
It cuts all the way into us,
where the soul and the spirit are joined.
Nothing in all the world can be hidden from God."
Hebrews 4:12,13 (NCV)

What Is the Bible?

"All Scripture is God-breathed and is useful
for teaching, rebuking, correcting
and training in righteousness."
2 Timothy 3:16 (NIV)

The Bible is a collection of books divided into two major sections. In the Old Testament there is history, laws and directions, poetry, narratives about individuals and adventure, and prophesy. All are about God and His relationship with human beings and all creation. The New Testament tells us about Jesus and his influence on all those around him, through his presence on earth as the Son of God.

The Bible was originally written one book at a time by different authors, some known and some unknown, over hundreds of years—all guided by the Holy Spirit to put The Word into writing. From Genesis to Revelation we learn of God's ancient and continuing relationship with humanity. At the very beginning of the Bible Adam and Eve's story tells us who we are and about our need for God.

We are obviously disobedient,
our natures are less than godly,
we're tempted easily and often, and we need to be forgiven.

When we read further we learn of God's continuing forgiveness, love, guidance, and protection.

Our sacred writings are the records of our ancient ancestors in faith as they sought to worship God.

The Bible tells us the history of many people through many centuries. Some of the individuals were important leaders for God. They heard God's word and led their people as God directed. They sought God's answers to all the problems and strife of their lives, and they waited patiently for His answers to be revealed to them.

The Bible is not only a history of these ancient people. It's a guidebook telling them and us how to live our lives as God wants us to live, how to have a close relationship with God, and how much God loves us and all His people. As we read about Cain and Abel, about David and Saul, about Jacob and the others, we find ourselves within the stories. We realize the Bible is about our disobedience, our lack of trust, our weak faith, our constant battles with our worldly desires. We also see our blessings, those we don't deserve which God gives us through grace and mercy.

It gives us answers to our questions. When we ask about God's existence, about His creative powers, His acceptance and forgiveness of our wayward behavior, His presence in our daily lives, we find answers in His Word.

"Surely you know,
Surely you have heard.
The Lord is the God who lives forever,
who created all the world.
He does not become tired or need to rest.
No one can understand how great his wisdom is."
Isaiah 40:28 (NCV)

We're told in the Bible that God speaks to us. And yes, He does. We see and hear these messages through His creation of nature, in the lives of godly people around us, in our worship of Him, in the daily miracles about us, and sometimes in the quietest moments of our lives. These are His audile and visual arts, His gifts to us. The Bible speaks of creation as part of God through glorious words spread throughout all its pages, and expressed joyfully in the poetry of the Book of Psalms.

The Bible is a Holy book, the Holy writ, a document presumed to be accepted by everyone as an indisputable authority. It's intent is to aid us in living our lives through the stories written by people who spoke for God as they were being directed by the Holy Spirit. We learn how the people of the Old Testament entered into a covenant with God. The Bible's courageous and heroic people show us today how to trust and love God. There are many who responded to Him through acts of reverence, portraying to us how we are to worship and revere Him.

The Bible is a teaching book,
telling us what we are to do.

We're to read it and then transpose it into action. What if, when it's time to prepare dinner, we find a recipe for a tasty casserole, one we know our family will enjoy and will be nourishing for our bodies. We read about the ingredients, the chopping and stirring, the oven temperature and the time required to bake it. Then we close the cookbook and forget it. At dinner time, will our family have the satisfying dish if we only read the recipe? No, and neither is God's will being carried out when we only read our Bibles. We are to *do* what we read.

Stories about God's presence in the daily lives
of Old Testament individuals were told orally,
generation after generation,
to be put into writing many centuries later.

Can you imagine these ancient people? Many were nomads surviving off the land. They frequently pulled up their tent stakes and moved to other locations, moving their entire extended families and all their possessions, to find water and pasture for herds and flocks of sheep, goats, cattle and poultry.

Think of being a mother during those days, of giving birth to new babies, preparing meals, washing clothes, gathering herbs and vegetation to eat, milking goats and cows, producing the clothing they wore by gathering plant fibers, spinning them into threads, weaving the threads into cloth, then constructing the garments by hand. They cared for sick children without the aid of doctors or medications, lived with wild animals nearby, were exposed to the elements of weather constantly, never expected diversionary entertainment nor had any choices related to daily needs. The severity of their lives, compared to ours today, is incomprehensible to us in its harshness—uncomfortable, unfulfilling, and truly frightening. It is through these people we first learn how God relates to humankind.

The first bits of the Old Testament were used by the priests as Scripture in the temple, then later in synagogues. Scripture is defined as *writing regarded as authoritative and inviolable.*[2] Most ancient people had previously worshiped several deities simultaneously, praying to gods of nature for rain and to gods of fertility for heirs. God expected them to worship only Him and to forsake all other gods. In Exodus 20:3 (NIV) we read what they were told, *You shall have no other gods before me.* It was this message they heard in the temple and synagogues.

It is the message for us today
as we unconsciously center our lives around money
and the things it will buy.

When we turn to the New Testament we learn that Jesus respected and taught from the old Scripture. This was hundreds of years after God had guided His nomadic people and spoken to them through Moses about their worship. Approximately four hundred years passed between the last passages recorded in the Old Testament and the beginning of the New Testament, which was all written within a period of approximately one hundred years. As we read the Bible, it may help in our study to acknowledge how different the two Testaments are in composition as well as in their messages, yet we'll discover how often the New Testament refers to words from the Old Testament.

"You will do well if you really fulfill the royal law
according to the scripture.
'You shall love your neighbor as yourself.' "
James 2:8 (NRSV)

The way Jesus taught about God enabled mankind to grasp of the meaning of the ancient stories and brought everyone closer to God.

The twenty-seven books of the New Testament were written about Jesus' life and his ministry and how he changed the lives of people forever, and about the development and establishment of the Christian church.

The first four books of the New Testament are the Gospels, which contain the parables of Jesus and stories about him. Later books relating the times after Jesus' death contain the history of the Christian church as it developed and spread. One of these, Acts, is church history; and twenty-one of them are letters written to people of the churches as they were first being organized. The last chapter is Revelation, a book of prophesy written during a time when Christians faced grave hostility from Roman authorities, and many were being persecuted and put to death. Now in our century, Christians are again suffering because of individuals and governments who seek to destroy their faith.

As we read the New Testament with our grandchildren we will teach them how Jesus lived and how he spent his days. His kindness to everyone, his understanding of people's troubles and hardship, his continued work for God even though this caused him to be unpopular with some groups of people, his love of God, the intense focus he had on his ministry—all these are stories intended to teach us, by Jesus' exemplary life, how to live and serve God.

Jesus' life personified all that's good. He personified God.

The Lord's Prayer (Matthew 6:9-13 and Luke 11:1-4), the stories of the Gospels (Matthew, Mark, Luke, John), the Beatitudes (Matthew 5:1-12), the parable of the Good Samaritan (Luke 10:30-37), and the birth of Jesus (Matthew 1 and 2; Luke 2) are appropriate, easily understood selections for our beginning Bible reading with our grandchildren. This material has meaning for everyone, young and old. The New Testament also gives us the story of the Lord's Supper and Jesus' prayer in the Garden of Gethsemane, then introduces us to the cross, the symbol of the Christian faith.

" . . . You will be right to depend on prophecy and take it as a lamp for lighting a way through the dark until the dawn comes and the morning star rises in your minds. . .
When men spoke for God
it was the Holy Spirit that moved them."
2 Peter 1:19,21 (The Jesusalem Bible)

The importance of the historical account in the Old Testament has great significance for all of us, for through it we learn about ourselves as God's people, whom God continues to guide, love, and forgive. The Word of the New Testament is a new message, but still the same message —still about God, whose supremecy, power, and love are revealed to us through Jesus. We may read it, ponder it, find newness in it each time we read it, and use it as a guidebook for further development of our faith in God. It, too, is the story of God's relationship to us, revealed in a way totally different from God's revelation in the Old Testament. Jesus' path to God is our path today. Another difference is lingistic. The original books of the New Testament were written in Greek, while the Old Testatment was written in Hebrew—with bits of Daniel, Ezra, and one verse in Jeremiah, written in Aramaic.

We're told that Jesus was educated as were other males of poor Jewish families of his day: He was instructed thoroughly in the Hebrew scriptures when he was a young child. His ministry began after he was baptized as an adult in the Jordan River by his cousin John the Baptist.

Throughout his ministry
Jesus was seen as rabbi and teacher,
one who accepted the authority of the Hebrew Bible
and followed its laws.

In addition to teaching, Jesus' ministry included healing the sick and performing other miracles. This brought many followers to him, and all this esteem caused him much personal trouble and anguish, leading to his crucifixion.

These words from Billy Graham's book *The Faithful Christian*[3] describe succinctly for us what the Bible is and why it was written:

God caused the Bible to be written for the express purpose of revealing to man God's plan for his redemption. God caused this book to be written that He might make His everlasting laws clear to His children, and that they might have His great wisdom to guide them and His great love to comfort them as they make their way through life. For without the Bible, this world would indeed be a dark and frightening place, without signpost or beacon.

"Scripture brought me to the gate of paradise, and the mind stood in wonder as it entered."
Ephrem the Syrian
Poet and theologian of the early church

People of the Bible

"He had begun his journey from Babylon
on the first day of the first month, and
he arrived in Jerusalem on the first day of the fifth month,
for the gracious hand of his God was on him.
For Ezra had devoted himself to the study and observance
of the Law of the Lord, and to its teaching . . . "
Ezra 7:9,10 (NIV)

As we read the Scriptures we learn how ancient people lived their lives so their days were pleasing to God. We've learned we're created to praise and serve God, and discovered the blessings in this as we read about individuals in the Bible who tried very hard to do God's will. They often disobeyed His laws, strayed from His guidance, and were miserably separated from Him; we also find them forgiven by God, continually led by Him even when they turned away, and loved by God whether they loved Him or not.

These are not just their stories, they are ours as well.

By helping our grandchildren meet some of these Biblical people and learn their stories about how they grew in their relationship with God, our young ones may be led to a stronger interest in the Bible. Knowing the names and stories of Biblical characters helps develop us in many ways.

Much of our secular education in the visual arts, literature, and world history is presented with an assumption that we know who these Biblical people are. If we don't know them we won't fully understand religious art, the messages of some literary pieces, the depth of musical renditions, nor the significance of some of the great historical social movements. Also, in our everyday life there are many maxims and cliches related to knowledge of these people. A simple example: when we read *the wisdom of Solomon* or *the patience of Job*, what meaning is there if we don't know Solomon or Job? Will *Job* be understood as a bit of work to be done because the pronunciation isn't known?

Noah's Ark games and decorative pieces for children's rooms are popular. Commerce is spreading the concept of Noah; however, if children don't hear Noah's story, they may assume these items are decorated with simple cartoon characters.

The following condensations about selected Biblical characters are provided as a starting place in telling our grandchildren about the Bible's people. You'll know the whole stories of most of these and will be able to fill out many details. For those you don't fully remember, find the Biblical passages related to these names and enjoy reading them again. Discover additional material about them and put together great stories that will be appropriate for your grandchild's age level and his experiences.

The information provided to us in the Bible is not given for us to read and quickly pass on to something else.

Each person and each portion has a lesson for us, sometimes many lessons.

Your job will be to look up the names of the Biblical persons in the concordance or index of your Bible so you may find the scriptural references to the specific individuals. (If you don't have a Bible with resource guides, purchase or borrow one soon. It's difficult to receive all the Bible has to offer without these helpful features.) Then, read these passages. Sometimes there are many verses in several chapters or even different books of the Bible in which these names will be mentioned. Let's become determined Bible sleuths and find them all. Next, put your stories together, using all you've discovered about what God is telling us through the lives of the Hebrews.

Study the maps in your Bible or in a Bible Atlas to learn where these people lived. Find the same areas on a current map or globe. What are the names of these nations and areas? Have you heard news lately about these old nations? Are you familiar with their most recent names? This information will help make your project exciting to older adolescents who may be studying world history or government at school.

Think about the cultures of Biblical times: lifestyles, economic situations, religious practices, rulers, and other influencing circumstances in the lives of these ancient people.

To the list of people described below, add your own favorite figures. Let's teach our grandchildren to search for stories about God's relationship with us.

ABRAHAM

Abraham is one of the most ancient men of God to whom we're introduced in the Bible. His name was Abram when we first read about him. There are other people in the Bible whose names are changed because of their encounters with the Holy Spirit.

Abraham learned about God from God. People of that time believed in and worshiped many gods. Abraham's own family and others around him were idolators. But God revealed himself to Abraham, who forever after that worshiped only God and led those around him to do the same.

Abraham was directed by God to leave his home, all his relatives, and his possessions, and to go to an unknown land. He had to believe in God and trust Him. He developed a special relationship with God, never doubting, and never turning back. This change in his life was difficult and harsh, and continued over many years. There were times of drought where he was and his search for food in Egypt developed into dangerous situations for both Abraham and his wife Sarah. But through his obedience to God, he became a man of total conviction. Though his concerns were urgent and difficult to bring about, in the midst of his struggles he never doubted God nor forgot Him. For his obedience, God promised Abraham ownership of an entire region over which his heirs would rule for all time.

Many years passed and Abraham and his wife Sarah became old without having any children. How would God's promise be realized without heirs? It was God's plan for them to have a son when they were very old. They named him Isaac. After Isaac had advanced into middle childhood, he and Abraham had an encounter with God on Mt. Moriah. Abraham's obedience here was proof of his faith in God. It was the strongest, severest proof of faith one can imagine. When we think of Abraham, we always think of Isaac and this story.

Centuries later Abraham's faith in God was upheld as *the* great example of faith by James (2:23) and Paul (Romans 4:3) as they retold the story in their letters to the new Christians.

Archaeological endeavors have revealed stone tablets covered with chiseled words and other artifacts from Abraham's location and time period.[4] Many artifacts of this period exist today, protected in museums and archives, dating the time of Abraham as a real time in ancient history. As we read about Abraham in the Bible we can feel this story's truth.

JACOB

Jacob was the second son of Isaac, and the grandson of Abraham. As an ancient method of inheritance, the oldest son in each family received the family's birthright. This was deemed to be the Promise of God's Blessing for this individual and was greatly revered. Jacob wanted it so badly that he talked his older brother Esau, who rightfully would have received this Blessing, into trading it to him. Then he went to his father Isaac, who was partially blind, to discuss the birthright. By impersonating his brother Esau, he was able to mislead his poor-sighted father into giving him the birthright.

Because of his deception and injustice against his brother, Jacob had to flee from his homeland, eventually settling in an area far away. During his escape, he dreamed of a ladder reaching to heaven as he slept by a pathway one night. In the dream he wrestled with an angel and recognized God's presence in his life.

After this Jacob was called Israel.

Jacob's life was not without troubles and disappointments. His father-in-law tricked him into marrying the older sister of his daughter Rachel, whom Jacob loved. He'd worked seven years for Rachel's father in order to marry her, now he must work seven more. Finally Jacob married Rachel and they had a family. Years later he returned to his boyhood home for Isaac's funeral, at which time he and Esau reconciled their relationship.

Jacob had twelve sons whose lineage eventually became the twelve separate nations of Israel. The names of the sons were Reuben, Simeon, Levi, Judah, Issachar, Zebulun, Joseph, Benjamin, Gad, Asher, Dan, and Naphtali. Throughout the Old Testament, and also in the New Testament, we find these names representing towns or regions. Look at a Biblical map and you'll find many of these names on it. Many of these places still exist and are found on current maps. Also, some of these names continue to be used today as males' legal names. How many men in your family have these Biblical names?

In Jacob's story we see God forgiving him many times, and guiding him to serve Him and bring about His purposes. Do you and your grandchildren see how God can use you just as you are? Is there a willingness in your family to do your best to learn God's purposes for you?

JOSEPH

Joseph, one of Jacob's twelve sons, was strongly disliked by his brothers. Because he was obviously the favorite of their father, his brothers made Joseph's life miserable most of the time, and after several years of this they sold him to some Egyptians. This was at a time when slavery was prevalent in that region and persons from one area could be sold or captured for enslavement in a distant area.

Many years passed, and many periods of distress and hardship were endured by the enslaved Joseph who was worked and often beaten. Worse than this were the painful memories of his family. He missed his father Jacob and his brothers, even though they didn't like him and had grievously betrayed him.

Much later, Joseph became a highly influential and powerful leader in the Egyptian kingdom when he averted famine throughout Egypt. Who would have thought this? He, who'd been sold into slavery.

During this time there was a famine in Jacob's land, so he sent his sons to Egypt to buy food. Through God's events, Joseph was reunited with his brothers, then with all his family. These stories demonstrate God at work in love, compassion, and forgiveness.

MOSES

Moses is seen in Jewish and Christian history as the most outstanding human being on earth during all the time before Jesus. He was a Levite (remember Jacob's son Levi?) whose very first days were threatened. His sister Miriam rescued him from dread danger, implementing Baby Moses' adoption by Pharoah's daughter.

In adulthood Moses was very close to God and frequently received messages from Him with specific directions. He was told to lead the Hebrews out of their Egyptian slavery; and across the Red Sea, towards the Promised Land. They, with Moses, wandered for forty years in the roughness of the wilderness. Many stories about God, Moses, and these people and their disobedience—their turning away and then turning back to God throughout many years— are recorded in several books of the Old Testament.

Young children enjoy the story of Baby Moses in the river among the reeds and about his growing up in the pharoah's palace. The impact of the stories, though, is seen in Moses' adult life. He was colorful, very human, a good man who was often disappointed in his observation of human nature. He followed God and did what God wanted even when Moses most likely was tired of doing the same things with the same people again and again. Can't you hear him asking, "Again, God? These people don't pay any attention to me. Surely I don't have to do this again." But he did. Moses was a true follower of God, an obedient man who fully trusted and revered Him.

Find the Ten Commandments in Exodus or in Deuteronomy and read them aloud with your grandchild. Then talk about how these are the same Commandments from which many of our current legal laws are taken. They make sense and make life better for all of us. God knew this would be so.

Our older adolescent grandchildren may be intrigued by the book of Numbers. In it are found two million ex-slaves who're wandering through the desert, following Moses whose only direction for when and where they were to go came from God. Today the trip from Egypt to the area they designated as their Promised Land can be made in nine days. It took the Hebrews thirty-eight years to make this trip. Along the way their faith matured, and we learn God's plan for them as we read this story.What does this say to us?

We may add interest for our older grandchildren by telling them about mummies of pharoahs found by archaeologists who've been able to date them to the time of Moses and the desert area where the Hebrews wandered. Local libraries will have picture books and more information about this.

DAVID

David was a young person when we first read about him in the Bible. King Saul was having grave trouble in his war against the Philistines. The biggest trouble was the biggest Philistine. This man was so huge and so mighty that Saul's military men feared him dreadfully. They thought of him as a giant—Goliath the Giant. Young David was a shepherd. He often used his sling and stones to protect the sheep in his care from lions and other wild animals. Many times he'd rescued sheep and had become very confident in his capability to kill lions and other fearsome animals by using his sling to aim stones directly to the animals' heads. Now he thought he could save King Saul's army—he would face Goliath with his sling and a stone. We know the rest of the story.

Years later, after King Saul died, David became the king of Judah. He was a very good king, one whom the people loved and served faithfully. He led them to work together to make their nation good, great, and righteous in God's sight.

David was a musician and a poet. While he was still quite young, David had sung and played the lyre to soothe King Saul, who was often disturbed by his kingdom's troubles—causing him to have headaches and sleepless nights. It is believed David wrote most of the Book of Psalms. Some are prayers, many are songs which were sung in the temple by the priests, and some we find today in our hymnals.

David's personal behavior eventually displeased and disappointed God; however, he sought God's forgiveness and remained devoted to God. We remember David for his exceptional reign as king and for his beautiful words in the Book of Psalms.

SOLOMON

Solomon was the son of David, who was king at the time Solomon was born to Bathesheba.

Solomon is known for his wisdom. He was a powerful king who led an era of peace and prosperity for God's people. He's also known for having built the Temple, which he began in his fourth year as king. It was to be the place of worship for all Hebrews. Solomon's literary skill continues to be honored regularly through the use of his songs and prayers in our worship services today. He's the author of three thousand proverbs, one thousand songs, and many scientific writings on botany and zoology. Three books in the Old Testament are accredited to him: Proverbs, Ecclesiastes, and Song of Solomon.

Individuals of The New Testament and Later Times

"*. . . As you have heard from the beginning,*
his command is that you walk in love."
2 John 6 (NIV)

As we continue through the Bible to study individuals of the New Testament we find the narrative distinctly different from that of the Old Testament. More than four thousand years have passed since the stories of Genesis originated. The book of Genesis covers more than 2300 years, the other thirty-eight books of the Old Testament contain the history of almost 1500 years, and approximately four hundred years passed unrecorded between the Old Testament and the New Testament.[5]

In the New Testament we no longer see individuals emphasized and portrayed one after the other, and stories of the lives and times of New Testament authors are essentially omitted as they write about the One who eclipses all other individuals of all time—Jesus.

As we read parts of the New Testament with our grandchildren, we may develop our own stories about Jesus' relationship with specific individuals who became his disciples, some who were healed by him, others whose lives were changed forever, and about his apostles.

From a large number of devoted disciples, Jesus selected twelve men. *These are the names of the twelve apostles: first, Simon (who is called Peter) and his brother Andrew; James son of Zebedee, and his brother John; Philip and Bartholomew; Thomas and Matthew the tax collector; James son of Alphaeus, and Thaddaeus; Simon the zealot and Jusdas Iscariot, who betrayed him.*

Most of these names are derived from Hebrew-rooted names of the Old Testament. Many are names still given at the time of birth to children today. The apostles were men in whom Jesus put his trust and they're honored by having other men carry their names through many centuries. Judas deeply betrayed that trust, and consequently we don't find other men named Judas.

**The parables Jesus told,
the Lord's Prayer, the Sermon on the Mount,
and other special portions of the New Testament
may be read over and over with our grandchildren
so they become familiar with these words.**

Let's teach our grandchildren how to find these Biblical selections, read them together, discuss their importance as the foundation of our faith as Christian believers, and use them in family devotions.

Our grandchildren may begin to internalize the concept of God's continuing guidance and His involvement in our lives when we bring their attention to family members or other persons they know whose lives duplicate the obedience, trust, and faith of the Old Testament people and that of Jesus' apostles and disciples. We may tell them about historical or contemporary individuals who've made our lives better by their own faith in God. Perhaps we've learned about them through their writing or through what others wrote about them. Think of Albert Einstein, Albert Schweitzer, Abraham Lincoln, Martin Luther King, and Mother Teresa. Choose from your own list of favorite spiritual people. Describe how they reflect the Word of the Bible, and how their messages are gifts for all of us, helping us make a difference in the way we live.

A lesser known group of people who've influenced people's lives are missionaries. Without missionaries on every continent changing the lives of indigenous people, Christianity would have been unknown in many lands for several centuries. Since Paul's unrelenting missionary work over much of the known world of his time, missionaries have continued to impact lives by dispersing God's Word throughout the world.

Perhaps you've known a missionary from your church or community, or someone in your family; or you may have read about missionaries and were intrigued by their lives when you were a child. The stories you tell may encourage your grandchildren to seek further information on their own. Describe how missionaries accepted hardship as a gift from God, how fear of the unknown became an exciting opportunity to share Jesus' love; how, when they were separated for years at a time from their families and friends, they made their homesickness acceptable by developing new friendships with persons who spoke languages they couldn't at first understand.

The stories of missionaries in earlier days are ours to tell—or our grandchildren may never hear them.

". . . what we have heard and known,
what our fathers have told us.
We will not hide them from [our] children;
we will tell the next generation the praiseworthy deeds of the Lord,
his power, and the wonders he has done."
Psalm 78: 3,4 (NIV)

How the Bible Came to Us

Throughout the centuries after Abraham's personal encounters with God the cultures and lives of people changed, sometimes slowly, other times rapidly, as influences outside and inside their own regions took over. Nations and the world changed; and people lived then, and live now, in many different circumstances—often from choice, and at other times because of pressures put upon them. Many used their time, energy, and other resources to satisfy their hungers and desires without God's involvement in their lives. But in all this time God never changed, nor has He changed today; and the Word of the Bible continues to be

God's message to us and for us.

The Bible's physical format changed throughout history as God used wise and good people to develop improved presentations of God's Word for us.

He guided selected individuals as He guided Moses, and today he continues to work through people to bring about growth, progress, better understanding, and deeper meaning in our lives.

Without these changes, this progression, and God's intervention, we couldn't understand the first information we have about God, which was inscribed on stone tablets in the language of ancient Hebrews. The Ten Commandments were not written in English.

From Abraham to this day the world has been changing and progressing from past years, with its progress given to us as a gift from God. This advancement helps us know more about God and our world and its abundance. As we're presented with new ways to study and learn about Him by scholars, theologians, archaeologists, and others, we're able to learn more about the ancient Scriptures. We all receive these blessings through God and should react with great gratitude.

"Go through the open gates with great thanksgiving; enter his courts with praise . . ."
Psalms 100:4 (The Living Bible)

The first inscribed portion of the Bible contained the Ten Commandments sent by God to the Hebrew people through Moses. The Bible tells us these Commandments were chiseled on flat stone tablets. During the earliest years these revered tablets were kept in the Ark inside the Tabernacle, which served as a nomadic temple. The people took the Ark with them as they moved about the wilderness, and later to the Promised Land.

Sometime later papyrus rolls were used for the lettering of God's messages. Papyrus was a writing material made from papyrus plants. Parchment, which was made by preparing animal skins (most often that of sheep or goats) as writing surfaces, also was used to record God's

Word. Eventually these rolls came to be called scrolls, and many years later, books as we know them were developed.

During Jesus' life our present Bible didn't exist. The New Testament developed as a result of Jesus' life, but it was centuries after his death before books about him, his teaching and his ministry, and his crucifixion and resurrection were written and selected to be included with the Old Testament to become The Holy Bible.

During this time *The Scripture,* as the Old Testament was known, was not in book form, but in scrolls, which were treasured and revered by the Hebrew people. Few copies existed, each being made by hand one at a time. These sacred Scrolls were so scarce only the Levites, or priests in later times, had access to them. Individauls didn't posses their own Scripture Scroll. When they went to the temple, or later to the synagogue, the priests read to them—that was their method of learning about God.

The words on the scrolls were meticulously inscribed by hand. The invention of the printing press with movable type occurred about 1450, hundreds of years after Jesus's life on earth. Think about our Bible. If there were only one Bible for all the people in our church, or only one for our entire extended family—grandparents, parents, children, and all the aunts, uncles, and cousins—how would we exalt our Bible? How much reverence would our family feel for this treasured writing?

For nearly two millennia, the Bible has been the cardinal text for Judaism and Christianity. . . It is more than a collection of ancient tales. Even before the canonical list of books considered sacred scripture or holy writ was established, the writings we now call the Bible were considered normative: they laid down the essential principles of how human beings should deal with God and with each other.[6]

The Oxford Companion to the Bible

For many years after Jesus' death, his followers continued to tell the marvelous stories about him. The oral tradition of telling the spiritual histories of ancient relatives had been used by the Hebrews for thousands of years before Jesus, and this same practice was continued long after Jesus' death to perpetuate the truth of his parables and of the events and actions he had experienced in his life on earth. His revelations about God were different and sounded more personal and loving than those of the early Scriptures, and his words which had been eagerly heard by the large crowds who followed him from place to place, continued to be coveted.

Eventually Jesus' followers searched for and gathered many of the letters written by Paul and his associates who were involved in establishing churches. These were cherished writings, describing to followers how they were to be Christian believers. By this time the leaf form of manuscript composition was in use and helped in the accumulation and preservation of these writings of Paul to the churches, as well as other material for the books which we now call The Gospels. All these together comprise The New Testament.

The small groups of believers who came together in Jesus' name after his death were the forerunners of our Christian churches. Their prevalent language during that time was Greek and the books of the New Testament were written in Greek, not Hebrew or Aramaic (Jesus' language, a sister language to Hebrew), even though most of the people involved were of Jewish lineage.

There were many years and much cultural change in the time between the Old Testament and these new writings about Jesus.

The four Gospels were reportedly written between sixty and one hundred years after Jesus' death. This time period overlapped with the time in which Paul wrote some of his letters and organized groups of believers. Paul had worked diligently, living with constant threats to his life because of his belief, in his determination to organize the churches. He was hounded at every turn by those who didn't want to see the church become a reality, and he was eventually taken to Rome and executed as a criminal after years of persecution.

After many years the need to provide the Word more comprehensively was felt by priests, Christians in the churches, and some of those who had access to the Scriptures. Many languages were spoken within the areas where the Gospel had spread, and translations into these languages would significantly benefit those who could read and understand God's Word. However, the work of translating from one language to another was slow and difficult. Think of working on this project word by word, day after day, for many years; and, when all the pages had been translated, there would be just one copy until scribes recopied it, day after day, one copy at a time.

The great effort executed throughout many centuries to protect and preserve the Bible as well as to translate it is difficult to fully comprehend.

We should learn about these people and their work, respectfully and with gratitude. They provided God's Word to us that we may understand His magnificence and the holy miracle of Jesus.

In Owen Chadwick's book *A History of Christianity* the stories of people whose lives were dedicated to translation and revision of the Scriptures are told in great detail. One of the earliest translators, a Greek named Ulfilas (341-383) had become a preacher through his Christian mother's influence. Ulfilas became a Christian bishop to the Goths, then fled to Bulgaria because of harsh and prevalent persecutions against Christians in his area. A devoted and learned man, he spent his next thirty-three years in Bulgaria preaching in Greek, Latin, and Gothic.

St. Jerome was a scholar of the same time as Ulfilas. He lived in an area near Venice but moved to Bethlehem to devote the rest of his life to working on the Scriptures. His eventual Latin version was called the *Vulgate,* which was considered the most influential of all Bible translations and is recognized still today as a sacred work.[7]

By the end of the fourteen century, John Wyclif's interest in the Church and its leaders inspired the translation of the Latin *Vulgate* into English. Following this, during 1525 to 1535, several scholars rendered seven or eight additional versions. In this period, William Tyndale, an English Protestant preacher translated the Bible into English. He finished in 1525, and though it was favored for a while, Tyndale was accused of perverting the sacred Hebrew Scriptures. Opposition to his translation became bitter, and his Bible was burned. Tyndale himself was burned at the stake in October, 1536, because of his work. Throughout history there have been many who, because they did God's work—or worshiped Him—were punished or put to death.

Troubles often besieged those who worked to translate or revise the Bible and threats were rendered to those who made any effort to make it more understandable. Often simply reading one of these revisions put early Christians at risk. During the 1500's several additional translations were produced, but in England Queen Mary Tudor (1553-1558) decreed that all printing of the Bible in English was forbidden, nor were existing English translations to be used in English churches. Because of her pressure on them, hundreds of Christians sought religious freedom by fleeing to other countries.

Many of the persecuted went to Switzerland. One of these, Robert Estienne, owner of the best printing firm in all Europe, moved his presses to Geneva. Here in 1560 he printed a New Testament in English, and soon after that he printed the entire Bible in English. Called the *Geneva Bible,* it's production had been undertaken and supported by English exiles, chiefly by William Whittingham, who had translated the New Testament into English in 1557.

The Geneva Bible was the first English version to have numbered verses.

Quickly becoming the choice of the people, the *Geneva Bible* was used almost exclusively for the next seventy-five years. William Shakespeare, who was at the end of his writing career, and John Bunyan, who wrote *The Pilgrim's Progress* used this version—as did the Puritans who fled to and settled in New England. They brought the *Geneva Bible* with them to the New Land.[8]

In 1568 Queen Elizabeth ordered English translations of the Bible to again be placed in all English churches and decreed that it should be read. This injunction resulted in still another English version, the *Bishop's Bible.*

In 1604 King James I ordered an English version to be produced, with its translation remaining as close to the Hebrew and Greek meanings as possible. Scholars and holy people worked diligently on this, and in 1611 a Bible dedicated to King James was published. It was known then, and is known now, as the *King James Bible, The Authorized Version.* With this authorized version then available, the previously frequent translations and revisions stopped. The *King James Bible* was used for more than two and a half centuries before any serious consideration of further revision developed.[9]

Today we still revere the *King James Bible*. Read aloud the beautiful passages and feel the depth of meaning and the harmony of the words in the rhythmic and almost musical arrangement of the language. Its powerful devotional character throughout the entire Bible moves us to the truth and knowledge of God as we read it.

Genesis begins with "In the beginning God . . ." then ends with ". . . in a coffin in Egypt." Between these eloquent phrases in the extraordinary book of Genesis is *all that is:* God, God's creation, God and Man, God's forgiveness and love, God's promise and Man's hope. We learn who we are and God's relationship to us.

The Psalms begin with "Blessed." What a wonderful word to look upon, to feel in our hearts. As as we continue reading the Book of Psalms we feel we are in the presence of God as it describes the wonders of God and His creation. The words of the Psalms are our personal prayers, our hymns, and our energy that moves us toward that which we desire to approach. They express our thanksgiving, our longing, our fears and dread, our sorrow, temptations, and guilt. And they provide us our joy, our laughter, our hope, and our love so that we may go forward in life.

"Blessed is the man . . ."
Psalm 1:1 (NIV)

"O Lord, our Lord
how majestic is your name in all the earth!"
Psalm 8:1 (NIV)

The *Authorized King James Bible* is more important to us than we may realize. It's been a part of our own and our ancestors' corporate and private worship for nearly four hundred years, and it continues to be used as a significantly special Bible.

Scholars, theologians, interpreters, writers, archaeologists, and others inspired by God continue to work diligently by using the *King James Bible* as well as other translations and resources to help in our study and comprehension of Biblical texts. Its absence from our lives would be a great spiritual loss.

Today we have Bibles with concordances, footnotes on each page, maps, indexes, material before each of the books, and revisions of Old English words to contemporary language. Now we can understand more fully the words of the Bible and the relationship that exists between God and His people. Also, we have available other books and resources, including audio tapes, videos, public lectures, motion pictures, and radio and television programs depicting or explaining portions of the Bible. God's word is readily available in many formats. All this material is available today to assist us in introducing the Bible to our grandchildren so their understanding and appreciation of it may be greatly magnified. It's up to us to select the most appropriate from all that is available.

"All scripture is inspired by God and is useful for teaching,
for reproof, for correction,
and for training in righteousness,
so that everyone who belongs to God may be proficient,
equipped for every good work."
2 Timothy 3:16,17 (NRSV)

". . . they received the word with all readiness of mind,
and searched the scriptures daily,
whether those things were so."
Acts 17:11 (KJV)

The Bible's Creative Influence on Man

The Bible's power to guide man and to move his heart spiritually is demonstrated by its influence on our art, literature, architecture, music, and other human endeavors. Reading about some of the great artists, musicians, and writers helps us appreciate the Bible's depth and inspirational qualities. Interest in visiting museums and galleries to see the works of specific artists, and to see and worship within magnificent cathedrals, may be instilled in our grandchildren. Visiting the areas where the original art and cathedrals still exist requires international travel; however, many beautifully illustrated art books are available for our grandchildren to learn about the works of early Christian artists.

Many frescoes and mosaics still exist in Rome, dating to the third and fourth centuries after the time of Jesus. Also in Rome, inscriptions and crude artistic markings remain on catacomb walls, some interpreted as Christian symbols depicting the beginning of Christianity. Our grandchildren may enjoy books related to these subjects and an on-going interest in searching for more information may be encouraged.

The inclusion of religious art as a part of the church began early within the new Christian faith. By 400 A.D. churches built for small groups of Christians frequently had paintings on their inside walls, depicting subjects from the Old Testament. Early in the church's history, there was much controversy about pictures inside the church regarding compliance with the commandment against graven images; however, the pictures came to be seen as aids to prayer as well as visual assistance in understanding the Bible for those who couldn't read.[10]

Following are examples of great artists whose works are known to most of us. Add to these your own favorite pieces and artists.

Our grandchildren will learn that God guides and inspires His people in diverse practices— and that we may expect His inspiration in our lives, for which we should be truly grateful.

With your grandchildren, find art books describing the work of Leonardo da Vince (1452-1519). Copies and reproductions of his *The Last Supper* are frequently seen in churches, in many homes, and as magazine covers and calendars.

Leonardo da Vinci painted *The Last Supper* on the wall of the Benedictine refectory in Milan. Though it's faded through the years, it continues to be restored and preserved, receiving much more care now than in earlier ages. In Napoleon's time, the large room containing the painted wall was used as an army store. Many years later, during World War II, the building was bombed and the ceiling fell in, but the wall with the painting was hardly damaged. It remains there today and restoration on it continues.[11]

Michaelangelo's *Creation* in the Sistine Chapel at the Vatican is another significant work of art which depicts the creation of God. It's painted in a glorious, grand scale, ascending across the ceiling of the chapel. Behind the altar of the chapel, Michaelangelo (1476-1564) painted *The Last Judgment*. He was the sculptor who carved *David* from a single block of marble, and also was poet and architect.

Among many others whose religious art portrays Biblical messages, and whom you might study, are Albrecht Durer, Raphael, Rembrandt, El Greco, and Rubens.

God's inspiration guided the hands of many people through their paintings, their sculptures, stained glass windows, great cathedrals, and through the music of composers such as George Handel (1685-1759). Handel wrote *The Messiah* and other masterpieces for churches.

There are also writers whose literary works have revealed the messages of the Bible.The most renowned, Dante is considered the greatest poet in the history of the human mind because of his great poetic masterpiece written about 1300 A.D. *The Divine Comedy* describes an order of the universe, an extensive moral, religious, and political system, a visionary excursion through Hell, Purgatory, and Paradise, and at the same time it defines the path of one's soul to purification. *The Reader's Encyclopedia* tells us that though we may understand the profound depth of Dante's creation, we must be able to read it in its original language to feel its wholeness and magic of the poetry adequately.[12]

Some of our grandchildren will be too young to grasp Dante's message; however, let's introduce them to the magnificent, the eloquent, the greatness of minds through which God works so that we all may have our lives enhanced and challenged. Learning of this poet, who wrote so beautifully about God's creation and His purpose for us that his work is known and appreciated for nearly seven hundred years after his death, stirs gratitude in our hearts for those who've given such gifts to us—and to God for their lives and for ours.

There are many creative people you'll think to add to the ones included here. God speaks to all of us and we respond in many ways, not only through art. He has guided physicians, scientists, technologists, theologians, teachers and many others who've endowed our lives through their wondrous contributions; and He continues to do so. As we study and read the Bible, He guides and provides us the wisdom to help us live daily with increased spiritual knowledge. Let's encourage our grandchildren to become interested in people past and present who have helped in our understanding of God's world, His power, His guidance for us and our places in this world. Let's help them become avid Bible readers by demonstrating our own interest in the Bible.

". . . and how from infancy you have known
the holy Scriptures, which are able to make you wise. . ."
2 Timothy 3:15 (NIV)

"Now choose life, so that you and your children
may live and that you may love the Lord your God,
listen to his voice, and hold fast to him.
For the Lord is your life . . . "
Deuteronomy 30:19,20 (NIV)

Helping our Grandchildren Use Their Bibles

As we prepare to read and study the Bible, we'll begin with prayer. We shall pray for God to illuminate our understanding, for when we understand the written Scripture, it is because of God that we receive His message, not because we are good students. Our prayers for our grandchildren will be that through their Bible study they will receive greater understanding of God and His purpose for them.

"The Lord will fulfill his purpose for me. . ."
Psalm 138:8

Planned instruction and study is required in anything we learn, and skills are improved by practice. Too often the knowledge we hope our children have regarding their faith and belief in God is left to chance. Would we leave to chance their capability to read? No! We would never do that. Our grandchildren deserve the same grave commitment to the sacred portion of their education that we'd give to any other portion of their education. Their Christian education is as important to them as all their other education combined.

**We may use the Bible as a manual,
a guide that tells us step-by-step how to live our lives.**

In describing the Bible in this way, we hope our grandchildren will perceive it as a useful book to be read daily. Because they'll handle it frequently, we'll teach them to have respect for the Bible beyond that of all other books. They'll learn about its composition—the Old Testament, New Testament, the Apocrypha, maps, indexes, concordances. Show them its divisions and how the chapters and verses are all numbered to help them find their way through its pages more easily. The first Bibles didn't have numbered verses. Think how difficult finding passages would be without this feature. We are grateful to God for the inspiration he provided to Robert Estienne for this beneficial inclusion in 1550.

Our grandchildren will soon understand the Scripture's content and the many centuries represented therein; the stories of ancient people whose relationships with God describe His awesome, loving, forgiving care for all of us; the poetry praising God; His laws, His directives; Hebrew history and records of their failures and successes as their faith in One God ruled their lives; the revelation of God's love through the birth, teaching, miracles, sacrifices, and death of Jesus; and the subsequent establishment of Christianity and churches.

Show your grandchildren your most cherished Bible, the one you received from your church when you were baptized or became a member of your church, a special one your family gave you, one you inherited from a family member, or a family Bible with all the family members' names with their birth and death dates. Or, show them the one your've used for years, in which you've underlined words and verses and jotted God's messages to you.

**Tell your grandchildren how you treasure your Bible
and how important it is to you.**

Visit a bookstore and choose a Bible for your grandchild, one which you both agree upon from the large number available, and one that is age-appropriate. If your grandchild is an early elementary reader, a large-print Bible may be easier to read, thus encouraging more reading. You may choose a study Bible which contains maps, definitive footnotes, descriptive inserts before each book, and other helpful material. Look through the bookshelves and survey the different choices available before you finally decide.Young children like Red Letter Bibles, specially marking Jesus' words. This practice is believed to have been developed by Louis Klopsch who was publisher of *The Christian Herald* in the late 1800's.[13]Whatever you choose, choose with care.You'll want this to be special, a gift from you that will always be cherished.

Reading inspirational material instead of reading the Bible itself is an inappropriate substitution. Nothing any writer may say about the Bible, or what it says about God, can take the place of personally reading the Bible.

The Holy Spirit uses writers and many people such as our pastors and Bible teachers to help us understand Biblical passages. Present all interpretive and supplemental information in addition to the Bible.

After your grandchild has her own Bible, talk with her about reading the Bible every day, perhaps setting a special time for doing so, as well as suggesting what and how much to read. Encouraging children to begin at the beginning of the Bible and to attempt reading it straight through is usually not a good plan. Your grandchild will likely do as many of us did—she may give up and quit trying. Show her special passages and tell her why you think they are meaningful to you. She may want to read the same ones over and over. Isn't that how we've learned most about God and Jesus; we've read and heard it over and over?

The following list is one provided by the American Bible Society many years ago.[14] Perhaps you've placed a similar list in the pages of your Bible sometime in the past.These lists are helpful for all of us and especially for anyone who is first beginning to use the Bible.

Where to Look in the Bible

To Find:

The Ten Commandments .... Exodus 20; Deuteronomy 5
The Shepherd Psalm .... Psalms 23
The Birth of Jesus ....Matthew 1,2; Luke 2
The Beatitudes .... Matthew 5:1-12
The Lord's Prayer ....Matthew 6:5-15; Luke 11:1-4
The Sermon on the Mount .... Matthew 5, 6, 7
The Great Commandments .... Matthew 23:34-40
The Great Commission .... Matthew 28: 16-20
The Parable of the Good Samaritan .... Luke 10
The Parable of the Prodigal Son... Luke 15
The Parable of the Sower.................. Matthew 13; Mark 4; Luke 8
Jesus' Death and Resurrection ....Matthew 26, 27, 28
..............................Mark 14, 15, 16; Luke 22, 23, 24. John 13 to 21
The Outpouring of the Holy Spirit ....Acts 2
That God provides ......Psalms 68:10; Isaiah 43:20; Jonah 1:17; 4:6-8

When You Are:

Placed in a responsible position ....Joshua 1:1-9; Proverbs 2
....2 Coninthians 8:1-15
Making a new home .... Psalms 127; Proverbs 17; Ephesians 5
.... Colossians 3:1; Peter 3:1-17; 1John 4
Out for a good time ... Matthew 15:1-20; 2 Corinthians 3; Galatians 5
Wanting to live successfully .... Romans 12
Feeling a grudge against another .... Luke 6; 2 Corinthians 4
.... Ephesians 4
Experiencing severe losses ....Colossians 1; 1Peter 1
Disobedient ....Isaiah 6; Mark 12; Luke 5
Needing forgiveness....................... Matthew 23; Luke 15; Philemon
Sick or in pain .... Psalms 6, 39, 41, 67; Isaiah 26
Feeling your faith is weak .... Psalms 126, 146; Hebrews 11
Thinking God seems far away............. Psalms 25, 125, 138; Luke 10

Leaving home .... Psalms 119; Proverbs 3, 4
Planning your budget and finances .... Mark 4; Luke 19
Lax and indifferent .... Matthew 25; Revelation 3
Lonely or fearful .... Psalms 27, 91; Luke 8; 1Peter 4
Afraid of death .... John 11, 17, 20; 2 Corinthians 5; Revelation 14
Sinning .... Psalms 51; Isaiah 53; John 3; 1John 1
Wanting to know how to pray .... 1 Kings 8:12-61; Luke 11, 18
Seeking a worshipful mood .... Psalms 24, 84, 116
.... Isaiah 1:10-20; John 4:1-45

". . . devote yourself to the reading of Scripture.
Be diligent in these matters; give yourself wholly to them.
Persevere in them."
I Timothy 4:13,15 (NIV)

As you read your Bibles, together or separately, you'll find your understanding is clearer and deeper, that more and more is revealed to you. Each time you read it, you change a bit, thus you are different in your knowledge and your nearness to God the next time you begin your reading. With wonder in your heart and mind, read the Bible asking "why, where, when, how, who, and what if . . ?" Give yourself time for answers to come to you. Teach your grandchildren to ask questions about their reading. Questioning is not doubting God's Word; instead, it is asking God for wisdom in your reading and understanding of His Word.

"Lord, tell me your ways.
Show me how to live."
Psalm 25:4 (NCV)

Activities for Chapter 3

Purpose

The following activities are planned to provide our grandchildren experiences to increase their knowledge and strengthen their developing perceptions as young Bible students by helping them understand why we revere and study this ancient book. They may gain a sense of how long ago these words were written, and how millions of people before us have read these same words and received the blessings, inspiration, and comfort we receive today from The Holy Bible.

1. Read the Ten Commandments with your grandchildren. Talk about the meaning of the words and the Commandments.Put each Commandment in today's context, making them pertinent to your grandchildren's ages, but keeping each one closely similar to its original meaning. The Hebrews recognized the Commandments as *the* Law, God's Law, and this remains so today—thousands of years later. Talk about which Commandments are also today's legal laws in our secular world and which ones are not legal laws that we must follow, but they do make our lives better when we observe them. Discuss how unsettled our world would be without these laws. Write a "Revised Version for Today" of the Ten Commandments, then discuss them. Encourage your grandchildren to memorize one of the Ten Commandments as it is written in the Bible.

2. Choose verses from the Book of Psalms to memorize for this week's mealtime Blessings. Read them together and discuss the meaning the words had when they were written, and the meaning they have today for your family. Is there any difference in the meaning? Many of the Psalms are short personal directives to us; and many are prayers and songs of praise to God. Find a Psalm you might read when you're seeking comfort and understanding, another that grandly praises God, and still another to read when you need to say, "I'm sorry; I'll do better."

3. Early Bibles were written in Hebrew and Greek. What if no one ever translated God's Word into English? Would we be willing to study diligently to learn Hebrew or Greek to be able to read the Bible this week? Ask your minister or a librarian to help you find a Bible written in another language. See how mystifying the marks on the pages are. Discuss how grateful we are to the dedicated and inspired people who worked long ago to make the Bible available in every language all over the world. Thank God for these people.

4. Go with your grandchild to a library to find religious art books. Look at the work of two or three artists you've selected to study on this day. Discuss how the artists portray the messages which God inspired them to paint. Think of other artists, your own favorite ones, or perhaps the artists whose works are on display in the library. Does God inspire other artists, even though they're not painting pictures depicting religious themes?

Does God inspire you to do some of the things you do? Will He inspire your grandchild? Of course He does, and will continue to do so. He puts power that doesn't come from us into our lives, that we may take advantage of it. Talk about this with your grandchildren. Help them learn how to take time to feel God's presence, to hear his messages, and to see His inspiration at work throughout the world.

5. Plan a pretend archaeological excursion with your grandchildren. Imagine you're members of an archaeological team searching for ancient artifacts. With preschoolers talk about how the old items you find can tell us how people lived in previous times. Perhaps you have an object which was commonly used in an earlier period, but which your grandchildren will not have seen used by anyone. An old flatiron is a good example and would demonstrate to them how women in our country seventy or eighty years ago pressed their clothes. This method of ironing indicates many other differences in life styles because there was no electrical power in homes at that time. Talk about how life would be for your family if there were no televisions, refrigerators, electric lights, motor vehicles, and other conveniences which we take for granted in our lives. Tie this information to your discussion about archaeological work as well as to the lifestyles of the ancient Hebrews.

You may encourage your older grandchildren to find books about the Dead Sea Scrolls, whose discoveries occurred in our lifetime (1947) by a young Bedouin goat herder named Muhammad Adh-Dhib. While searching for a lost goat, he stumbled upon a cave with a very small opening whose treasures will be discussed and studied forever. The cave was filled with pottery jars containing religious scrolls, some of which are thought to be a thousand years older than any other biblical manuscript. They had been placed there for safe keeping by members of the Qumran community during a time when their very existence was threatened by Roman persecution, making their lives unbearable (in 68 A.D.).

Included among the scrolls was a copy of almost all the book of Isaiah. In addition to the alert and curious goat herder who discovered the cave, God led the archaeologists who've protected, restored, and preserved the material found in the cave, and the scholars, interpreters, and theologians whose continued work and interpretations provide us with the messages found in the scrolls.

Help your grandchild find *The Dead Sea Scrolls*, written by John Allegro in 1956.[15] Allegro, an archaeologist with firsthand knowledge, tells the exciting story of the discovery and the extensive work of the archaeologists, other scientists, and many others who worked diligently for so many years to bring information of this achievement to us.

Talk about how the scientific field of archaeology helps us learn more about the Bible and its people and about our faith and God.

6. Plan to bury a time capsule containing elements of your family's life. Have a family meeting to discuss the items you'll each place in the capsule. These items will indicate what your family deemed significant during this time period to whomever is present when your capsule is unearthed years later.

Choose several items, perhaps one or two from each family member. Each one might write a secret letter telling about his or her personal life, what each does for recreation, describing school, favorite foods, special events of the present year, and exceptional difficulties and achievements in each life.

A waterproof box designed to be stored underground or a large plastic jar which can be sealed to make it waterproof will serve as your capsule. You may wish to seal your items in plastic bags for further protection.

When you have your capsule as you want it, decide where you'll bury it. Perhaps you'll decide to bury it in your yard instead of that of your grandchildren. Also, involve the adults in a discussion about an area where wash-outs or excavations are unlikely, and where a tree or another feature will remain to mark the place so you'll always remember where it is. There are many instances in the Bible in which God gave directions for marking a spiritual location so his people would remember it.

Finally, set a date when you'll do your archeological dig to retrieve your treasures. Talk together about how old each of you will be at that time. Where will each one live? If you bury it in your yard, will this be the "family home place" where they will always gather for many years in the future? This discussion may uncover the need to develop family goals, to learn more about the family's heritage, and also to make more plans for the capsule. You may plan a ceremony when everyone will come together in the specific year you've selected to dig up the capsule. You'll see the items you placed there, remember them fondly, or perhaps realize your personal growth over the past years. You'll read the letters to each other and remember the time when you planned this event. There are so many frequent changes and discoveries today that we can't imagine all that will have changed during this time. All these years your grandchildren will have grown physically, mentally, and spiritually. Discuss the great reunion you'll have when you come together to unearth the capsule.

7. Help your grandchildren understand that God is available to all of us at all times and that we may seek His loving presence in our lives during times of need as well as at times when we are exuberantly happy and want to express appreciation. This activity is one for quiet conversation, closeness, sincerity, and absolute honesty. Discuss the times Jesus withdrew from everyone to think and plan and pray.

Talk about the numerous times God helped the Biblical people and the great deeds many of them accomplished with God's help. Tell them how God comforted you during a sad time when you felt all alone, and how God helps us grow through sadness and disappointment. Let them know God builds our self-confidence by giving us courage and guidance, and that He supplies our needs, though He may not do so immediately.

Discuss with your grandchildren what they'd do if they *knew* they couldn't fail. What would you do with your life if you knew without any doubt that you wouldn't fail? Doesn't God help us, doesn't He keep us from failing? Don't we always have our needs met? Encourage your grandchildren to go for their dreams, to ask God to be with them in their life goals, to help them sort through their ideas and develop those that are pleasing to Him. Pledge your support to help them reach their goals. Can you help them in any better manner? Lives lived this way are very different from materialistic lives without goals—and without God.

8. Choose a Psalm that was often sung in ancient times. Reading it aloud together, feel the flow of music even though you're not singing. Imagine ancient people in temples or synagogues chanting or singing these same words.These words of worship are a part of our heritage. Let's respect them, honor them, and praise God by using these Psalms often in our daily prayers or Scripture reading.

9. During Old Testament and New Testament times men and boys were allowed in the synagogues to study and learn about the Scriptures; women and girls, slaves, tax collectors, and certain unacceptable men were not. Discuss the differences in customs of previous times. Tell your grandchildren of changes which have taken place in your lifetime and how change improved your life and the lives of those around you. Talk of the progression of God's work in His world and how many aspects of our present culture will be different when your grandchildren are grandparents. Remember that through all changes and all the years that pass, God is the same forever.

10. Visit a large old church on a day during the week and ask someone to show you the Bible on the altar or any other Bible that's special to this particular church. There are many treasured Bibles kept in churches around our neighborhoods which are unique enough to be museum artifacts because of their ages or significance. Perhaps you'll make a great discovery by finding an unusual Bible in your search. Pastors and church staff members will usually be very happy to assist you in learning more about the Bible.

11. To share our faith with the youngest members of our families, we may hold these new babies in our laps as we read our Bibles and daily devotions and pray aloud. What we do now is what they'll do later. Seeds planted and deeds enacted while our grandchildren are babies will awaken their spiritual depth early in their lives. When we pray aloud in their presence for God's guidance for them, God hears us, and that which the very youngest child hears is implanted in his heart. Why would we delay, thus deny, these wee ones just because they're small?

12. Help your adolescent grandchild become an interpreter of the Scriptures. Encourage him to study diligently, then to choose his

favorite Psalms, ones that speak especially to him. Suggest that he might rewrite a favorite Psalm. Instead of David pleading for deliverance or thanking and praising God, help him change the ancient terminology to today's words so the Psalm expresses your grandchild's feelings about his life. He may also rewrite the Beatitudes so they reflect circumstances today. This should be done only after careful discussion.

"Ask, and it will be given to you; search, and you will find; knock, and the door will be opened for you."
Matthew 7:7 (NRSV)

Note

This material is not intended for grandparents to use just as it is written in sharing with their grandchildren. Instead, it's written for adults and aimed at jogging *our* memories and stirring *our* interests in the Bible that we then may develop a hunger in our grandchildren which can be fed only through Bible study. We want them to know the Bible is pertinent to their daily lives, and that in many ways it is through God's Inspiration in others that we live as fully as we do. By this, we're endowed by Him even when we don't know Him fully. God's love is revealed through the Bible; and His plan for His people is there.

WORSHIP

Chapter Four

". . . the true worshipers will worship the Father in spirit and truth, and that time is here already."

John 4:23 (NCV)

Chapter Four

WE WORSHIP GOD

"Come, let us bow down in worship,
let us kneel before the Lord our Maker;
for he is our God
and we are the people of his pasture . . ."
Psalm 95;6,7 (NIV)

As our creator, God expects us to worship Him with unrelenting commitment and faithfulness. God's commandments, given to His people many centuries ago, required them to love and worship Him; and today these commandments still are the requirements for God's people, wherever we are.

God redeemed the Israelites again and again, and instructed them to worship and serve Him. God spoke to Pharaoh, admonishing him to let His people leave Egypt; then He directed Moses to lead His people through the Red Sea and eventually to Mt. Sinai where they were given the Ten Commandments. Their deliverance from Egypt was to be commemorated by worshiping God at designated times throughout the year; and over many centuries the Israelites continued to worship God regularly in many different lands, and on many special occasions.

Many of the Psalms were written to be used in the worship of God. By accompanying them with music, their words were often sung to exalt and praise God. Adoration is a fundamental part of worship. Today in worship we praise and adore God, often using hymns and Psalms to aid us in this part of worship. In ancient times the Levites, who later came to be the Levitical Priesthood, were selected by Moses through God's direction to lead the Israelites in worship when they came together. The Levites read the Scriptures and sang the Psalms as God's people listened attentively with awe in their hearts.In the beginning this practice helped to establish God's laws, as well as to lead the people in praise and worship of God.

Later, Jesus taught us that we may worship God without the assistance of priests, that we ourselves may seek God and reach out to Him in worship, prayer and contemplation as provided us through Jesus's life, teaching, and resurrection.

**Jesus also taught us to pray, to love, to serve,
and to forgive one another;
to help the needy, and to heal the sick;
and he urged us to use the Scriptures of our ancestors
that we may learn God's purposes for us.**

After Jesus' death, his followers established churches, providing places for worship where the Scriptures could be heard and Jesus' life and teachings could be honored and remembered. Today we still respect and abide by the ancient commandments given us in Exodus and Deuteronomy, and we strive to live by the life and teaching of Jesus.

Throughout both the Old Testament and the New Testament, we learn our purpose in life on earth is to worship and praise God. To worship God is to honor and show reverence to Him, to respect Him, to exalt and glorify Him. God's ancient people were expected to dedicate certain times to God for corporate worship when all the people came together to sing, pray, read the Scriptures, and praise and adore Him. We're expected also to devote regular private times in which we show Him gratitude, pray, read His Holy Word, and praise Him.

This chapter will guide our thoughts about why we worship God, how we worship Him, the parts of worship services, the church and its people who worship, and how we're brought into God's presence through worship. In addition to corporate worship, we'll think about how personal, private worship enhances both our individual and family lives.

Study in this chapter with our grandchildren may lead to their recognition of God at work around them, creating a desire in them to participate in regular worship of Him. As always, begin this section by asking God for His guidance as you share your faith with your grandchildren.

" . . . So they sang praises with gladness
and bowed their heads and worshiped"
2 Chronicles 29:30 (NIV)

Why We Worship

"Hear O Israel: The Lord our God, the Lord is one.
These Commandments that I give you today are to be upon your hearts.
Impress them on your children . . . "
Deuteronomy 6:4,6,7 (NIV)

St. Augustine (354-430) wrote, *Whisper in my heart, tell me You are there.* We stir within, longing for God. So we sing praises with gladness and bow our heads and worship. We want God, we seek God, we worship God. All, the essence of our life.

We worship because God expects it; and, because we're seeking a secure haven, one that is beyond our capability to supply. Not only do we worship God as we must, but because as humans our restlessness, our greed for more, and our dissatisfaction has no end. Through worship, we seek spiritual restfulness and self-acceptance through God.

Even though we worship God, we're unsure about our knowledge of Him. We're earthly beings, finite in all parts of our lives; yet, we try to communicate with God. We think of God's majesty and power, His boundless creation, the mysterious and transcendent aspects of God. We ponder His holiness. The Bible teaches that He is not in the wind, the earthquake, or the fire, but in the silence of the gentle air.

How can we stretch our minds to comprehend God's great dissimilarity to man?

Romano Guardini in *The Art of Praying* defines our uneasiness about God's vastness when he writes, *God's holiness makes us uncomfortable.*[1] And James Hillman in *The Soul's Code* says, *Thinking of God not as man but as a 'something else' disturbs minds that mistake comfortable thinking for clarity of thought.*[2] We try to reach into God's realm when we worship, consciously keeping our minds on spiritual heights, and trying to lift our minds and souls to zeniths we've never experienced. When we worship we're obeying God and seeking greater understanding, a closer relationship and acceptance, yet realizing that as the Book of Esther tells us, God being God, His thoughts are beyond our ability to comprehend fully—His mind is beyond our ability to grasp completely.

"God is spirit,
and his worshipers must worship him in spirit . . ."

We don't fully know God. He is completely separate from all others, and the very concept of His being is beyond the rational thought of man; thus, through our worship we involuntarily approach Him with great awe. We give way to Him, completely surrendering to His Being, opening ourselves to His will which we'll accept through His grace. That is why we worship.

And that is enough; however, we also receive personal benefits through worship. By focusing on God in worship we realize how much we appreciate and love Him.

The constant love of God changes our bad times to appreciation for the opportunities available in all times—good and bad.

By praising and honoring God for his greatness and purity, we become greater and purer than we were. Praising God becomes an act of self-help, and we begin to look at ourselves in terms of what we can be.

By placing our thoughts on God, our spirits are revitalized. We feel God's presence and acknowledge His guidance in our lives. We have more enthusiasm for our work and daily responsibilities, and we can put our fears aside.

Though we most likely will never fully understand the concept of God, by worshiping Him we may have religious experiences which interpret *the feeling which remains where the concept fails.* (Rudolf Otto, 1869-1937, *The Idea of the Holy*).

All these benefits and the growth we experience, are gifts to us from God. They are available to all who worship Him. Let's make an extended effort to assure that our grandchildren receive these gifts and the great benefits produced by them.

Worship is an every day, on-going duty. Duty will turn to adventure, joy, anticipation, and fulfillment when it's practiced regularly. D.L. Moody, the founder of the Moody Bible Institute, wrote many years ago, *A man can no more take in a supply of grace for the future than he can eat enough today for the next six months, or take enough air into his lungs at one time to sustain him for a week. We must draw upon God's boundless store of grace from day to day as we need it.*

Our grandchildren's spiritual growth happens one step at a time, and by returning day after day to the fundamental teachings of the Bible, to daily prayer with God, to meditation or periods of solitude as they listen to God's messages within them, they receive God's benefits. Our society's troubled environment denies these benefits to children, but we grandparents can turn this around.We can go with them to worship services and help them with their daily devotional practices.

"It is written, 'You shall worship the Lord your God,
and Him only you shall serve.' "
Luke 4:8 (NKJV)

"It is to be a witness between us and you and
the generations that follow, that we will worship the Lord
at his sanctuary . . ."
Joshua 22:27 (NIV)

What Is Worship?

"As the heavens are higher than the earth,
so are my ways higher than your ways
and my thoughts than your thoughts."
Isaiah 55:9 (NKJV)

Worship expresses our awe of God; it is our acknowledgment of God's Immanence and His Holiness. It transmits our respect and reverence for Him, and our longing to be owned by Him. In worship we're in an altered state of consciousness, realizing we're in the presence of the Spirit of God, feeling at one with heaven and earth, body and soul.

Worship is very personal. Organized religion has structured worship services, with each church's service being different from all others, though most are very similar. There are orders of worship which include specific rituals and formulas, rules of procedure, and strict, polished language. The purpose of all these procedures is to help us in our worship of God. Though we join with others in worship, each person retains his individuality and approaches worship in his own personal manner. Persons side by side in pews are worshiping unlike each other.

In worship, there are moments of silence. These times are not simply the absence of sound; instead, they can be felt in our hearts and souls, full and warm, speaking to us.

Worship is not just what we do on Sunday,
all dressed up for church.
Instead, it's a full-time endeavor as we strive to fulfill God's purpose for us.

Not only do we worship God on Sunday, for we are told to put aside the Sabbath for rest and worship, but we also worship Him through our thoughts and actions every day. Kindness towards others, caring for God's earth, forgiveness of another's callousness, helping the needy and sick, embracing healthy habits as a life style—all are acts of worship in small personal ways when we're directed in our hearts to do them.

"We praise (worship) God not to celebrate
our own faith but to
give thanks for the faith God has in us."[3]

We'll experience many moments of worship as we constantly search for the sacred in our ordinary lives. These moments aren't defined by times and places as our church services are, so we must commit to consciously seek them or create them, and to recognize them. At home in the quiet of the morning, in the late afternoon after work as we rest on the porch, and at night as we say goodby to the day and goodnight to each other—in all these times God's grace pronounces itself, bringing us to worship. On hanging up the phone after our daily call to an aging parent, we feel overwhelmed by God's love and care for His elderly children, and for all of us.

When we feel grateful
and express thankfulness to God for our abundant lives
and his guidance in our troubles,
at this time we're worshiping God.

Though worship for us is internal and not necessarily plied with physical manifestations, let's not equate worship with "good feelings." Simply because we feel "up" during a time of worship doesn't necessarily mean we have offered God our will, wholly in truth and honesty, and are effectively worshiping Him. Neither, however, does it mean we're truly worshiping God just because we feel "down" or "out of it." We are to offer to God all we are and all we have in our worship of Him, praising and adoring Him as we do this.

None of this is to diminish the importance of worship in church. We should thank God frequently for the important work and diligent presence of the multitude of churches in our country. It is through them we have been enabled greatly in our knowledge of God.

Corporate worship, within the fellowship of believers,
may benefit us through its potentially therapeutic features:
aesthetics, familiar rituals, music, prayer and meditation,
distraction from daily routine, relief of tensions,
endowed wisdom and education,
and occasions for socializing with like souls.

Many of us have experienced deep spiritual moments during formal worship services. The music, the beauty of the stained glass in the sanctuary, the words of priests or pastors, the ritual, and the ceremony itself help guide us in our worship of God. However, participation in formal worship services does not eliminate the need for our connection to God through our sincere private worship of

Him. Guardini says it best: *This connection is substantiated only through a Christ-like consciousness displayed by us in our every day physical, mental, and emotional lives.*"[14]

Worship is a serious, dedicated act. It comes as close to being godly as we will ever attain, and it is exceedingly difficult within the daily melange of pressures and responsibility. Faithful, honest effort and dedication must be assigned to our plan for worship. It must be seen as a necessity in our lives, deserving the best we have to offer. Slighting our efforts of worship leaves us cheated and empty by our own hands. Let's eliminate the unnecessary rush of our lives and concentrate on the necessary. Help your grandchildren understand just how much they will receive by sincere worship, and help them learn to faithfully worship God in honesty and truth.

Honoring the Sabbath

"Observe the Sabbath day by keeping it holy, as the Lord your God has commanded you."
Deuteronomy 5:12 (NKJV)

"If you call the Sabbath a delight and the Lord's holy day honorable,
and if you honor it by not going your own way and not doing as you please or speaking idle words,
then you will find joy in the Lord."
Isaiah 58:13 (NIV)

The Sabbath is an ancient, hallowed gift to us from God. In the Old Testament we find many references to the Sabbath and how we're to observe it. The Ten Commandments tell us we're to work six days and rest on the seventh; and we're given strict directions against working on the day God set aside. Exodus gives us these words: *Remember the Sabbath, to keep it holy.*

By the time of Jesus's influence, the Israelites were expected to follow the law regarding the Sabbath so diligently and strictly that frequent conflicts erupted. The priests' interpretations disallowed any work to be done on the Sabbath, so arguments resulted regarding the needs of desperately sick people, accidents that needed attention, and other singular occasions in which immediate attention was required. Jesus' answer to them, *The Sabbath has been given to you; you have not been given to the Sabbath,* allows us to apply spiritual consciousness to the interpretation, urging us to help others and assist in times of crisis with acts of Christian love and by remaining connected to God throughout.

This gift of the Sabbath is truly a gift in every way. It is freely given to us and we may do with it as we wish. We may disobey God's command or we may do as we're directed and honor the Sabbath.

The Sabbath is a weekly, customary opportunity to do for God, to honor Him, praise Him, remember Him, give the day to Him, study His word, thank Him, and worship Him.

Observing the Sabbath is a significant act which usually we may carry out without hardship or deprivation to ourselves; however, we are often negligent and selfish about giving this day to worship. Still, God does everything for us, beginning before we're put on this earth and continuing into eternity, moment by moment.

The observance of the Sabbath on Sunday, the first day of the week instead of the seventh day, began by the end of the first century CE. Early Christians observed this day as the Sabbath and it continues today; however, there are some Christians, notably the Seventh Day Adventists, who still follow the Old Testament directive.[5]

Some feel the Sabbath is not a specific day of the week, but any day that is set aside to honor God as they're able. Our most beneficial view of the Sabbath is to be all inclusive, honoring God's claim on us to worship Him through corporate worship at its specific, regular time and place, as well as practicing our private worship on other days and nights as we feel appropriate through God's guidance.

In our frenzied lives we cram even our leisure time full of hurried activity, continuing to be doers, staying busy.

God calls on us not to do, but to be.

On the Sabbath we're directed to be quiet, still, calm, meditative, thoughtful, and worshipful. God directs us to rest on the Sabbath; and for most of us restful Sundays will be very welcome.

Perhaps we can become calmer and quieter in all parts of our lives just by setting aside the Sabbath to worship and think about God. He's silent, though He's never away from us. Think about this reality: When God seems absent, He's actually present. In His silence we seek His guidance and assistance in our trials, failures, sins, and hardships. We may also praise and adore Him through our silence. Jesus frequently went off alone to pray and to be with God. Silence is good! Let's discuss this with our grandchildren. Teaching them to "hear silence" and to feel its depth prepares them for worship experiences.

As we develop our inner lives and greater faith in God, we'll come to cherish the blessings of solitude and quiet, and the time we devote to worship. An anonymous writer suggested that we have been given our inner lives to care for just as God gives an infant to a mother to care for. Let's treat them tenderly, nourish them, and help them grow.

Worship of God helps us comprehend more
and to see ourselves differently.
We begin to discover God's purpose for our lives.

Let's help our grandchildren set aside time for worship so they may learn God's plan for them before they become adults. What a difference this will make in their lives as they become parents.

Do you remember the Sundays we spent as small children? Tell your grandchildren about the days before shopping malls. Stores and businesses were closed on Sundays, there were few people on the streets —just those strolling, enjoying the quiet and restfulness. Traffic was minimal and the entire atmosphere was peaceful.

In the years following the opening of malls and shopping centers, stores were allowed to open on Sunday afternoons, after people had attended church worship services. And in today's hurried and harrassed world, many stores are open twenty-four hours every day, seven days every week. The latest complaint of those who do go to church on Sunday is the scheduling of children's competitive sports events. They begin early on Sunday morning and continue throughout the day. For many families now, there is no difference in one day from all others. Every day is filled from morning until evening with wild rushing. There is no calm, quiet, meditative moment in which they stop to praise and worship God.

It's our responsibility as God's people
to set aside time to worship God,
who has given us all we are and all we have.

We can't return to the time when stores were closed and when the temptation to shop on Sunday didn't exist. But we can decide that on the day we worship God, we will not do the work of the other six days. We can plan ahead, so that our Sabbath is calm, quiet, contemplative, restful, good for our spirit, with time for the worship of God. Could it be that the people who take time for quiet and peace in their lives also have the energy and frame of mind to control their lives?

Perhaps on Sundays after church we'll visit someone who's ill or lonely, write a letter to a distant relative or friend, or take a long walk in the woods where we can hear the sounds of nature. Will this change be so difficult for us? Do we really want to do it? What do you think God thinks about our attitudes? Won't our grandchildren find true childish delight in setting aside a day for doing God's things?

Children benefit greatly when they're
provided quiet time as a gift and not as punishment.
We do them a great favor to introduce silence
as a benefit to them—
time when they may think about themselves, their families,
their good times, their need to change, their hopes,
what God may want them to do,
how He will help them through troubles.

Things to think about are endless, and what if your grandchildren never have an opportunity to think about any of these? Try it and see what happens to your grandchildren. All we could ever accomplish on Sundays will be overshadowed by the benefits for our grandchildren.

"Too late have I loved you, O Beauty,
so ancient and so new,
too late have I loved you."
Lamented by 3rd century philosopher St. Augustine

"All your children shall be taught by the Lord,
And great shall be the peace of your children."
Isaiah 54:13 NKJV

Why We Worship at Church

Sunday mornings are special times for many individuals and families as they gather to worship God in churches across our land. Sunday worship has been a part of our country's heritage since the earliest colonies were established. The freedom to worship in America is absolute and profound. We're so sure of its continuation and its ready availability that we take it for granted. Years, perhaps even generations, pass without our having one conscious thought about thanking God for our religious freedom.

Many of us have totally disregarded
our ancestors' excessive hardship and sacrifices
as they fled from religious persecution,
crossed a perilous ocean,
and came here to utter barrenness
to live a harsh and difficult life
so that they might worship God freely.

All of us today benefit greatly because churches exist in our country. Worship experiences, Christian education, and the social services provided for members and their surrounding communities serve us even if we are dissidents who never, ever attend church or participate in any way with them. We're influenced through the people with whom we associate daily who are part of a church in our communities. Churches make all our lives better through their connection to God.

In our worship we're recipients of all those who have extended the knowledge of God to us: Abraham, David, John the Baptist, Paul, the Bible prophets, the Bible's authors and translators, musicians and artists, architects of great cathedrals, scholars and theologians, our ancient ancestors, our families, and Jesus —all who have directed us to God.

We have not come to this place by ourselves. We must remember to be thankful for each one who's helped us, though they may remain nameless to us.

Worship is personal interaction with God. We recognize the opportunity to grow spiritually as we dedicate ourselves to serve Him. Our inner self becomes prepared for worship through confession, Scripture reading, thanksgiving, dedication, devotion, and prayer. Through the church we have opportunities to be led in our worship of God in ways we by ourselves may not perceive. Also, the church provides ways in which we may serve God.

When we come together in corporate worship as a congregation, we usually participate in a formal worship service with an order of worship delineating different steps of the service. Quiet organ music may be heard upon our entering the sanctuary, where we are encouraged to sit quietly in meditation for a few moments. The music and the beauty of the sanctuary enhance our worshipful feelings.

As the service begins, candles may be lit by acolytes. A choir introit, liturgical readings, congregational singing of hymns, prayers by the pastor and the Lord's Prayer repeated by the congregation, offertory music as the offering plates are passed for our tithes, a doxology as gratitude for what we've just given and what we've been given, Holy Communion when we share the bread of our Lord Jesus Christ, portions of scripture read aloud, and the minister's witness through his sermon are all possible parts of a formal worship service. A benediction sends us back into the community to serve and live until the next Sabbath.

"Remember the law of my servant Moses . . ."
Malachi 4:4 (NIV)

Through this form of worship we often experience a deepened connection to God, feeling that we've received more and done more. We feel so uplifted we may sometimes misinterpret our feelings. Let's not think that we've made God better, larger, nearer, or higher. We cannot raise God. He raises us. We're raised when we praise God and celebrate our faith, and we give thanks for the faith God has in us.[6]

Worship is for us; it's a gift from God. God gives, and we receive. We do not do it for God; we do it for ourselves, that we may be lifted and connected to God. God doesn't *need* our praise and worship. We need it; so we praise Him, and do with our lives what He expects. If we don't, He doesn't change. If we do, we do change.

"I will praise you, O Lord, with all my heart;
I will be glad and rejoice in you;
I will sing praise to your name, O Most High."
Psalms 9:1,2 (NIV)

Elements of Worship

Soren Kierkegaard (1813-1855), the Danish philosopher who based his belief on faith, knowledge, thought and reality, said, *Worship is a drama with different parts— speaking and singing, praying and giving money, baptizing and eating bread and drinking wine—all for the delight of God.* This is our worship service, a presentation of prayers, offerings and celebrations. Can we make all of life such as this?

Each single part of the worship service is meaningful when we study its place in the service and its message for us. All the parts woven together as a completed worship service assist us in connecting with God in our personal worship of Him. Corporate worship, when we all come together to praise and worship God, is deeply meaningful for us, tying each of us to each other in fellowship and belief, as well in the care and concern for each others' souls.

The treasured rituals of formal worship services reassure us and soothe our longings for a spiritual connection to God. We depend on the tangible and liturgical symbols which are part of our tradition of worship to carry us forward in our spiritual journey and provide emotional security for us. That's why older members of congregations sometimes object to changes in the order of worship or other rearrangements. Symbols bring us together and provide a safe haven.

Sanctuaries are filled with symbols, beauty, and items (such as baptismal fonts) not seen in other places. They are proper places for worship; however, let's not separate God from our daily lives and place him only in church. The God of the sanctuary is the same God of the boiled-over beans and tired crying children, of too many bills and too little money, and of the weeds and stones of the garden.

In many churches we find stained glass windows depicting Biblical history and Christian symbols. The Christian cross is seen throughout the interior—on the altar, in the architecture of the sanctuary which often is built to form a cross, in windows, on the hymnal covers, the altar cloth, the ministers' robes, choir robes, at the ends of pews. There are so many crosses in our churches we don't see them all. The simple beauty of the sanctuary feeds our souls and lifts them towards God.

"The human soul needs beauty
even more than it needs bread."
D.H. Lawrence, English writer and poet

If your grandchild has not been to church recently, take him one weekday to sit quietly in a pew with you. Look around the big room at the beautiful windows, the symbols of faith you can see from your seat, the cross on the altar—any of its features that make it different from other rooms. Talk about what you see and how you feel in this place.

"Every young man who listens to me
and obeys my instruction
will be given wisdom and good sense."
Proverbs 2:1 (The Living Bible)

There are some practices in corporate worship which also build our spiritual lives. All of these are not included in every worship service. Designated as Christian sacraments, they are Baptism, Confirmation, Holy Communion (or the Lord's Supper), Foot-Washing,

Ordination, and Holy Matrimony. Not all churches celebrate all as sacraments; however, most churches do include at least one as a part of their worship at times. A sacrament in Christianity is any of certain rites instituted by Jesus and believed to be means of grace.[7] *The Book of Common Prayer* describes a sacrament as *"an outward and visible sign of an inward and spiritual grace."*

"God is spirit,
and his worshipers must worship
in spirit and in truth."
John 4:24 (NIV)

The Church as God's Institution

". . . make a sanctuary for me,
and I will dwell among them."
Exodus 25:8 (NIV)

The multitude of churches spread across the expanse of America today represents the fulfillment of God's directions to the Israelites. Chapters 25 to 40 in Exodus provide detailed instructions for the construction of the tabernacle which the Israelites were to build. It was to be a portable shrine in which the ark would be placed, constructed to be dismantled and reassembled as they moved from place to place. The tabernacle was where God was present with his people and where he communicated with them. The Israelites were diligent and reverent about the care of the tabernacle, moving it with them wherever they went, and always seeking God within it.

Today's churches are quite different from the tabernacle and the ark that was hoisted onto men's shoulders and moved throughout the wilderness, though we must remember that God is still the same. It is He who directed Moses, and it is He who directs us.

The function of our church is to assist us in communicating with God. That's the reason for its existence. We're assisted by the church through Christian education for us and our children; through worship services that teach us by scriptural readings and sermons, witness, prayers, and music; through projects that give us opportunities to grow as we serve mankind; and through righteous people—pastors and church members who are wholly dedicated to God. Also, there are many relationships within the fellowship of the church membership, some with members whose lives lead us further toward God and others who challenge our self-concerns, arrogance, pride, and selfishness.

The church is not a perfect place—and most likely God doesn't care about that. His concern rests in our personal spiritual growth and our truthful connection to Him.

The church can help us with these.

The Christian church did not exist during the life of Jesus; however, it was because of Jesus that it exists today. Within a few years after the death of Jesus, the disciples began to be called "Christians" after Paul and Barnabas founded a church in Antioch.[8] Earlier, many of Jesus' followers had been called "Believers" because they continued to talk about his teachings, and they sincerely believed in and practiced what he'd told them.

Through diligence and sacrifice the Christian church soon spread beyond the area in which Jesus lived and traveled. Remember this was before the days of motor vehicles, communication systems, and printing presses.

Some who worked to establish churches were put to death; others were thrown into primitive prisons to die, and most were ridiculed, denounced, and threatened. These churches were for everyone who believed in the teachings of Jesus. Jews, Gentiles, and many who previously practiced pagan religions now came together in this new Christianity, causing much political upheaval. To learn the Biblical history about the early church read the Book of Acts in the New Testament—the first book of church history.

The church we attend each Sunday, or the ones we pass by, did not come into existence easily. Therefore, we should be thankful for the first people to be called Christians, as well as for those who came to our country seeking religious freedom three centuries ago. Our churches are here for us through much personal sacrifice and struggle.

For hundreds of years around the world there have been many different Christian churches with different theologies, dogmas, practices, and interpretations of specific details in the scriptures. However, before the fifteenth century there were hundreds of years in which sameness of dogma and the word of the pope reigned. Most Europeans were under the rule of the respective kings or other rulers of individual countries, whose duty was to protect their citizens from warring neighbors, while the church (the pope) educated them and cared for the poor. This practice subsequently broke apart under pressures for reform and the doubt and mistrust brewing from within the church, which had become very powerful and wealthy.

In the sixteenth century the Reformation set people free from the bondage they felt under one church. Now they could study the Bible, seek truth, and express their beliefs in new ways in their personal encounters with God. Out of this eventually came all the denominations of Protestantism, and over the years more change and progress was experienced within the Catholic church also. Read about Erasmus and Martin Luther in an encyclopedia or history book.

Churches provide for us in many ways, most of which we take for granted. Thomas Moore in *Re-Enchantment of Everyday Life* lists several situations in which we're assisted:

> *"Aside from the churches, we have no positive,*
> *adequate means of dealing with death,*
> *the meaning of accidents, nature, intuitions,*
> *rites of passage, sacredness, holy places,*
> *ethics and values, and education."*[9]

Through churches, members come together as a community of faith, each person worshiping God in an individual manner. As members of a church, we look upon the congregation as our own small community where we may receive assistance when we need it, and where we're loved unconditionally. These people compose a spiritual body, sharing in a communion of faith and love. In Matthew 18 we read, *"For where there are two or three gathered together in my name, there am I in the midst of them."* Let's not take this for granted, nor dismiss it lightly. We go to church because God is there.

There are many people who feel they don't need to go to church, and they say this doesn't mean they don't believe in God nor ever read the Bible. They say they can feel reverence, awe, and love for God without church attendance, and that yes, God still loves them and they love God. And what they say may be true, but the Christian fellowship is bigger than that.

A letter from a reader in the April 1997 issue of *Family Fun* objected to a previous article in which. . . *a family eschews organized religion, but found spiritual fulfillment by establishing a small library in a homeless shelter.* Choosing small closed-ended projects that make us feel good is not the same as "taking in the stranger." The reader commented that when we fail to provide ongoing religious guidelines for our children, it's like saying, *I'm not going to instruct them in the proper way to treat others.*[10]

Children of families who don't attend church
may lack Christian education,
the wholeness of the Christian faith,
the witness of the community of believers,
the environment created when one or two are gathered,
the spirituality and beauty of worship services,
and God's presence within.
THERE ARE MORE THAN THESE—
MAKE YOUR OWN LIST

If our grandchildren never attend church worship and/or Sunday School, is it possible that on some future date they may come to us with the news they've joined a spiritual group—because all human hearts seek God in many unconscious ways. There are many paths available for our young people today, and many of them are very questionable, and some are frightening. But if our children have had no direction given them, how can they determine the right from the wrong when they're approached by a seemingly righteous one who makes promises? How will we feel when we tell them, "Our family has always believed in God. We used to always go to church." Then they may ask, "Why didn't you take me?"

Our souls long for God. And when our grandchildren haven't been introduced to Him, how do they know when the gods being introduced to them are false? Perhaps they are instructed to be secretive about their new "faith."

As we work with our grandchildren and encourage them to attend church with us, let's become intensely aware of *why* we're doing everything we do. Why do we worship God? Why do we believe in Him? Why is the church important in our lives? Why are we concerned that our grandchildren know God? Why are we planning now to lead our grandchildren through our faith to the knowledge of God?

Rushing about daily in a society steeped in moral decay, we find ourselves dedicated to many secular activities about which we haven't asked, "Why am I doing this? How does it impact my life? What will happen to me if I stop doing it?" Asking "Why?" to everything that takes our time and other resources, and answering ourselves honestly, will set our feet on new paths.

As we teach and encourage our grandchildren in their developing faith, let's help them find the sacred in all of life.

We may share with them more of our faith from day to day as we see their own faith developing, their love for God and their interest in following Jesus' teaching growing stronger. They will be changed, and so shall we. And, if we find they have an interest in attending church—and if we go with them because children need the support of adults—this connection to God will be manifested in all they do all their lives.

May God's blessings fall on you and His guidance place your steps on His path as you continue sharing your faith with your grandchildren.

"Blessed be the Lord, our God,
from everlasting to everlasting.
Amen and Amen"
Psalm 41:13 The Oxford Bible (NRSV)

Activities for Chapter 4

Purpose

The following activities will help introduce, or reintroduce, ourselves and our grandchildren to the love and care to be discovered within the community of believers in our chosen churches. Through them we experience the various parts of worship services and realize how they bring us closer to God, feeling grateful for all that is bestowed on us by Him; we will identify the opportunities for soul growth available in the church. Let's encourage our grandchildren to establish an ongoing devotion to God and connection to Him throughout their lives.

Please develop these activities to fit your own interests and beliefs through resources you have available in your communities. If you are not affiliated with a church presently, talk with a friend, a family member, or simply visit a church and tell someone there about your project with your grandchild. You'll have a very agreeable resource available to you, and you'll feel truly welcome to return often.

"O Lord, we pray for the universal church,
for all sections of your church throughout the world,
for their truth, unity and stability,
that love may abound and truth flourish in them all."
Lancelot Andrewes (1555 - 1626)[11]

1. Have a family discussion about simplifying your lives. Ask each family member to list all the activities they perform each week. This includes meal times, personal care, family chores, school and after school activities, weekend projects, as well as times alone by yourselves. After everyone has made a list, discuss all of them briefly to determine where your time, energy, and money are spent. Has there been any time designated during the week for God? Are you finding joy and personal fulfillment in the time you're spending in everyday activities?

After sharing your lists with each other, prioritize them, putting the most necessary ones at the top, and the unnecessary ones at the end of the list. As you talk about what you're doing, are you discovering activities that may easily be eliminated? Can you re-prioritize so you have more time and are able to do everything easier and with more joy for you? Are you willing to eliminate activities which have no redeeming value for your lives?

When you've completed the changes you want to make and have a new list from which you'll arrange a new schedule, discuss the need for each family member's commitment to the new list.Talk about sacrifice, dedication, striving, cooperation, development, benefit, advancement in knowledge and capabilities, and love for each other. When the project is totally finished and everyone understands and agrees with the changes, spend some moments in closing, signifying that this is an important move in your family life. At the end of this time together, hold hands and thank God for your family's decision and ask His guidance and His blessing as you incorporate the changes into your lives.

2. Decide to make your next Sunday a true Sabbath. If you do or do not attend church, spend the day quietly, thinking about your lives and God's interest in them. Don't do strenuous household chores, catch up on work you didn't complete last week, or get a headstart on the upcoming week. Don't shop or do commercial activities.

Some activities you may find more conducive to making the Sabbath special are: resting; thinking of God and Jesus, being reverent in your thoughts of Him; enjoying nature, expressing gratitude for the natural gifts you're given by God; reading the Bible, hymns, or poetry; listening to quiet music; thinking about each member of the family and how blessed each one is to have these brothers and sisters, these children, these parents and grandparents; visiting someone who's lonely or sick; writing letters to friends who seem to have no joy in life at this time; conversing with each other or playing quiet board games; reading books you enjoy; taking a walk or playing with your pets outdoors; going on an outdoor picnic. What a great day your grandchildren will have.Include them in planning your Sabbath, but don't overload the day with too many choices from these suggestions. Make it very different from the other days of the week so they'll begin to think of the Sabbath as being very special.

3. Usually formal worship involves ritual and liturgy. Help your

grandchildren plan a short worship service to use after dinner one evening soon. Decide what parts you want to include.There are no rules you must enforce; however, the length needs to fit your specific circumstances. For a responsive reading in which your youngest grandchildren may participate read Psalm 136. This liturgical Psalm alternates verses with the same refrain, "His love endures forever (NIV)," and your younger grandchildren will feel they're part of the service because they're saying the words, and these are words which they can understand.

4. The Angelus is a Roman Catholic devotion in which those who hear the ringing of the church bells bow to say a special prayer designated for this devotion. When the Angelus is being observed, the bells ring and prayers are recited three times a day—at six a.m., noon, and six p.m. Artist Millet's painting *Angelus* depicts persons bowing where they're gathering grain in a field, as they hear bells in the distance beckoning them to prayer.

Find a print of this painting and read more about this devotion. Talk about the reverence and devotion of those involved with your grandchildren and how such a life would be different from our lives today.

Is there a way you might develop a prayer time with your grandchildren? Will all the adults participate? It isn't necessary to adapt this concept fully, but the pure beauty and reverence of this devotion has benefits for us. Decide how you might use a bell, or a cd of chants or quiet organ music, or some other sound which you might incorporate into a "call to prayer" for you and your grandchildren.

The purpose of this is to have them stop whatever they're doing for just a moment and say a prayer of praise and thanksgiving to God, one you may choose together before you begin. Agree upon the time you'll do this, perhaps one or two times each day. You may want to plan this for just a week. Later, discuss how you felt each time you stopped and remembered the words of the prayer, saying them to yourself and to God. Decide if you want to continue, and change whatever needs to be changed to make it more meaningful for everyone.

5. Older adolescent grandchildren may develop greater appreciation for the Bible and for our heritage of worshiping God by studying materials related to the Dead Sea Scrolls. You'll find information on this subject in public libraries and in church libraries. Also, the pastors

of your church will most likely have books relating to this subject and may have been enrolled in seminary classes covering this material.

Only since 1947 have these materials been available, for that is the date of the first discoveries at Qumran, an area near the Dead Sea. Through scientific investigation dates of origin have been determined as between 250 BCE and 70 CE. Today the artifacts of the discoveries are kept and protected in the Rockefeller and Israel museums where some of the major Scrolls may be seen by the public. All are available to qualified scholars and others interested in studying and researching the Scrolls.

These ancient scrolls consist of the text of the Hebrew Bible. Every book in the Old Testament is represented in these discoveries except the book of Esther, with most of the book Isaiah being represented.

Learning about the Dead Sea Scrolls may lead your grandchild to additional interests: theology, liturgy, and rituals of our ancient forefathers; archaeology and anthropology; ancient history; early printing methods and materials; and geography are fields of information which may entice young people to study further.

Discuss this great discovery which we read about in our newspapers as it was occurring in the late forties. Think about what would have been available to us if television had been more advanced at that time—it was in its infancy and on-the-spot reports were not possible. Consider how the discoveries have enhanced our understanding of the biblical material they contain, after many scholars, scientists, and theologians have investigated and studied them for almost a half century.

Find pictures and stories about the Dead Sea Scrolls. Make copies of pages with pictures of the Scrolls and the jars in which they had been stored. Help your grandchild start a journal or notebook in which to collect information related to this project.

6. Discuss with your grandchildren the work and responsibilities of pastors and ministers of our churches. Talk about their call by God to become ministers, their training, sacrifice and commitment to the ministry of God. Talk with a minister about his work and his dedication to it, his daily responsibilities as the leader of his church and as a leader in the community.

After your visit with a minister, have your grandchildren become ministers for a day, doing the work they've learned about. They will spend their day praying, helping others, reading the Bible and other inspirational material, writing a sermon, going to hospitals and nursing homes. Their thoughts will be completely on others, not on their own interests.

At the end of the day, ask them to discuss with the family how they felt as ministers for God; difficulties they had in staying focused on their interest in others instead of themselves; what they learned about themselves and any changes they may make in the future in their lives. When did they feel God's presence during the day? This discussion will be your grandchildren's witness to others about God and His day. Talk about witnessing.

7. Always be in search of beautiful liturgy and ritual, regardless of the denomination or faith which it represents. Worship with your grandchildren at many different churches, participate in their rituals and liturgical readings, enjoy their hymns (some of which may be different from the ones of your church), compare their order of worship and the parts of worship to that of other churches with whom you are familiar. Look at their sanctuary and the altar area and think about how their symbols represent God. Remember that where one or two are gathered in His name, God is there. Think about our religious freedom and how important it is to us individually so there may be different ways to worship God and to represent Him.

8. If you don't already know, discover which church in your area has the largest pipe organ. Arrange with the church to visit with your grandchild when the organist practices for the worship service. Ask her to tell you about the organ and demonstrate its great sounds for you. On the following Sunday attend that church's worship service. Listen especially to the beautiful music provided by the organist and the organ.

When you travel to large metropolitan areas, worship in large churches where there most likely will be large pipe organs. Arrive early so that you may hear all the music played before the service begins. Another way to appreciate this great religious music is to buy cd's of organ music, perhaps that of London's Westminster Abbey Choir, the Mormon Tabernacle Choir, or others. These massive choir organs have been dedicated to God, and are used for centuries in worship to Him.

9. If you don't have a hymnal, borrow one from a local church and use it for a week to read the words of hymns, sing them, and have your musical children play them as you all sing the words. Study the composition of the hymnal. There will be many hymns whose words have come from the Book of Psalms and you'll discover divisions throughout the hymnal separating the hymns by topics. The names of poets or authors as well as those who composed the music are stated, as are the dates of the music. Memorize a hymn you like and sing it every day for a week. Plan to memorize other hymns in the future. Learn the words to the following hymn:

Take Time to Be Holy

"Take time to be Holy, Speak oft with thy Lord;
Abide in him always, and feed on his Word;
Make friends of God's children, Help those who are weak,
Forgetting in nothing His blessing to seek.

Take time to be Holy, The world rushes on;
Spend much time in secret With Jesus alone;
By looking to Jesus, Like him thou shalt be;
Thy friends in thy conduct his likeness shall see."

This hymn, based on I Peter 1:16, is an example of scripture used in the wording of hymns. It was written by William D. Longstaff, who lived from 1822 to 1894. The music for these words was composed by George C. Stebins (1846-1945), and since then multitudes of people have sung it during the past century. It's found in a section of the hymnal called Prayer and Aspiration. Discuss how these words guide us on our path to love God and help others.

Note

Worshiping God and living as faithful people is our purpose throughout all the days of our lives. Our grandchildren's understanding of God's plan for them is established through their capability to worship God. God has a plan for them.

Will we help our grandchildren grow closer to God so that they are able to more fully recognize the path they are to follow? Introducing them to worship experiences, to the fellowship of believers, to the majesty of corporate worship in which God is the focus through music, scripture, prayers, liturgy, and other religious manifestations provides for them the parts of their spiritual development that we cannot personally provide. Our task is to introduce them to this form of worship; God will do the rest as we continue living our faith as an example before them.

LIVING OUR FAITH

Chapter Five

"By wisdom
a house is built,
and by understanding
it is established . . ."

Proverbs 24:3 (RSV)

"It takes wisdom to have a good family,
and it takes understanding
to make it strong."

Proverbs 24:3 (NCV)

Chapter Five

LIVING OUR FAITH IN THE WORLD

Truly Living in Faith

"Since we live by the Spirit,
let us keep in step with the Spirit."
Galations 5:25 (NIV)

As God's people, we're capable of following God's guidance every day in all we do, say and think. Because we are not puppets of God, we reason and choose what we do as part of our mindful living; therefore, we must truthfully want to follow Divine direction—continuously, and with dedication.

"It's a sad day when you find out that it's not accident
or time or fortune but just yourself
that kept things from you."
Lillian Hellman (1905-1984)

Whatever our circumstances, or those of our children and grandchildren, nothing should prevent our sharing our faith in the world. We are called to honesty, not to success and ease; to love and service, not to materialism.

Grandparents and others who recognize God's presence about them can build spiritually eventful lives whether they live in gated villages or slums, whether they are known as celebrities or unknown to most.

"The real moment of success is not the moment apparent to the crowd."
George Bernard Shaw (1856-1950)

When we look at everything in our lives as being of and by God we find that we all have the possibility of glorifying God; each thought, the ability to lift us and those around us through prayer; each time together, the hope that we are Christ to all about us, and they to us—then we realize the potential for living faithfully in the world.

The world is filled with choices, and God allows us to choose. The potential for faithful living is at risk of our choosing against it.

All about us, in all we do, that which may affect us positively or negatively, is waiting to be chosen by us. What we take into our lives—bad or good, poison or nurture—is accommodated by our choices. Our spiritual life at the time, or the lack of it, sets the tone for our decision making.

"You must observe them [laws] diligently, for this will show your wisdom and discernment to the peoples . . ."
Deuteronomy 4:6 (NRSV)

Wisdom to live is ours to develop, to nourish from its infancy to glorious full development. Children need help in laying this foundation for their faith—the foundation of being capable to think clearly, to plan their days before they proceed, to pray for guidance, to realize their need for knowledge, to have courage to do what God guides them to do, and to do this humbly, compassionately, and kindly.

Wisdom will help our grandchildren focus on that which is valuable to their life in God and far-reaching to the ends of their lives, with consequences affecting school and study, choice of careers and marriage partners, all life's hard decisions, and all relationships.

Wisdom comes to us from God, through the Bible and study, other books and printed materials, worship, prayer, the people around us, and the religion we follow.

We also gain wisdom through the hard lessons of our bad choices.

Aristotle tells us that whatever we learn to do, we learn it by actually doing it: *Men come to be builders by building, and harp players, by playing the harp. In the same way, by doing just acts we come to be just; by doing self-controlled acts, we come to be self-controlled, and by doing brave acts, we become brave.* And, we add, by living as God's faithful in the world, we become faithful.

The Bible leads us to faith through wisdom and directs us in righteous behavior, attitudes, thoughts, words and actions toward all others. These two steps—developing wisdom, and doing God's will in the world—comprise the manner in which we're to live in the world.

Living in faith is expressed through continuously and consciously growing in wisdom, and through doing God's will in the world.

Our work with our grandchildren involves our attitudes, our virtues, and our character. If we ourselves need restoration, we may benefit through our work with our grandchildren, strengthening our wisdom and faith. Wisdom is God's way of making our spiritual lives more deliberate and responsive.

"Wisdom is bright, and does not grow dim.
By those who love her she is readily seen,
and found by those who look for her."
The Book of Wisdom 6:12,13 (The Jerusalem Bible)

Our Being, Our Self

"Wisdom is a fountain of life to one who has it . . ."
Proverbs 16:22 (NRSV)

Living each day in families with friends around them within their communities; going to school, gym and other activities; responding to nature's changing conditions; experiencing times of sickness and health, celebrating birth and mourning death; enduring disappointments, loss, and failure, our grandchildren spend their days in the world. Through this they establish the foundation for their lives, and work on becoming who they will be as adults. It is within these and other daily living experiences that our grandchildren may learn God's will for them and learn to live in faith in the world.

Most of us have no saints nor monks, ministers nor mystics in our immediate families; our homes are neither sanctuaries nor convents, nor are our lifestyles protected and secured from all trials, enticements, seductions, and other spirtual perils. Most of us live fully in the world with only ourselves through God's guidance to keep us on His path.

We grandparents must show our grandchildren how we may incorporate and project a Christian life each day amid the activities, personalities, responsibilities, enticements, and all else that makes up a normal secular day. We all must live our faith in the world about us.

This chapter captures the worldly and helps us move faithfully into it, working to become more for God, for our families, our friends, our communities, and ourselves.

"I am the Lord, I have called you in righteousness.
I have taken you by the hand and kept you."
Isaiah 42:6 (NIV)

"Praise be to the Lord,
for he showed his wonderful love to me . . ."
Psalm 32:21 (NIV)

Grandparents may help their grandchildren identify God's path for their lives and demonstrate serving in the world as a part of His will for us.

The development of virtues, values, goals and other beneficial attributes are taught in the secular world in various ways. In recent years we've tried to provide children enough self-esteem to benefit them in the future, as if self-esteem is readily available in shrink-wrapped packages. Self-esteem as a value has taken the place of character. When outstanding character is developed, there's no need for concern about one's self-esteem.

"He that has light within his own clear breast
May sit i' th' center and enjoy bright day."
John Milton (1608-1674)

Successful and virtuous people are not so because of who they are but because of how they live. It's imperative that compassionate, loving adults teach children how to live in the world. Many children—some who are very young—are finding their direction through their peers, instead of through caring adults. At very early ages, many children are taught how to live in the world on the street, some following the lifestyle and mentality of gang leaders.

We should intervene when our grandchildren choose friend groups who denounce parental guidance, declare their independence from their families, move about in groups, set distinct dress codes, develop their own speech patterns, hang out together every day after school, participate in activities they know their parents disapprove, and are not fully accountable to their parents.

Children cannot benefit by being brought up by children. We have seen this in the tragedy of teen pregnacies. God planned for families from the beginning of time. There have always been families; no child has ever been born without parents.

". . . You will be ever hearing but never
understanding;
you will be ever seeing but never
perceiving."

When Jesus spoke these words, he was talking to those whom he knew lacked discernment. His spiritual guidance simply passed by these people without their hearing it. We must prepare our grandchildren so this doesn't happen to them. As they grow older, they will recognize the difference between a life of faith and a life without faith. From the foundation we help them develop they will grow to choose God's road for their journey.

"My business is not to remake myself,
But make the absolute best of what God made."
Robert Browing (1812-1889)

We will teach our grandchildren to live fuller, to love generously, and to be couragous in following God's Way. Our work with our grandchildren may be a breakthrough for us, too. George Eliot's words provide hope for us when she says, *"It's never too late to be what you might have been."*

Teaching our grandchildren how to live in faith guides
them to see more fully, to hear more deeply,
to concentrate, discern, seek understanding,
desire wisdom, become aware of the music in their hearts,
to feel the breath of all nature joining their breath—
All as feeling God's presence in their lives.

Our Beginning; Our Families

". . . it is important that the tales which the young
first hear should be models of virtuous thoughts . . ."
Plato's *Republic*

". . . all the families of the earth
shall be blessed."
Acts 3:25 (NRSV)

All of us are members of families. We have relatives—people who look like us, walk like us, talk like us, stand erect or stoop like us. Our skins may be smooth and dark, or light and easily freckled; our hair, thin and light colored or dark and thick. We have parents, and grandparents, aunts and uncles, and cousins many times removed. Also in our families there are those who're not truly related to us but are members of our families through marriage. How many of us dearly love Cousin Daisy who married our real cousin Frank, who brought her into our family more than forty years ago?

Family! How extraordinary is the meaning of this word. It means comfort, delight, warmth, care, gifts, understanding, acceptance, and love to most of us. Family also means responsibility, reciprocation, trust, honor, sharing, respect, and unconditional love. For the adults in the family, teaching and exemplifying are duties assumed to last throughout our children's youth; whereas the reciprocating duties of our children are obedience and respect.

Parents are responsible for teaching their children values to live by: moral values, essential relationship skills as values, spiritual values, choices as values, and love values. We could easily put all of them under spiritual values, encompassing all in one; however, here we will emphasize each area so we may help our grandchildren realize the worth of each and the growth that may come from understanding the greater depth of parental responsibility.

"For children to take morality seriously
they must be in the presence of adults who take
morality seriously.
And with their own eyes they must see
adults take morality seriously."[1]
William Bennett

Moral is something we are, not something we have. We have the opportunity to help our adult children exemplify moral living in front of our grandchildren in their homes and in ours, and in the world about us. We know what is moral; we don't have to study this.

We only need to live morally each moment to help our grandchild develop a moral center within her being. Our list of moral values includes honesty and truth, kindness, compassion, courage, self-control and all the beneficial virtues of moral living. We should also include impulse-control as well as self-control, delayed gratification as a companion to unselfishness, and frustration tolerance as verging with compatibility.

Our grandchildren see greed, self-interest, indulgence, laziness, disobedience, dishonesty and other negative behaviors all about them. Except for the youngest of our grandchildren, they know the difference just as we know it. They will choose to live righteously if the adults around them are living positive moral lives.

Our teaching morality develops its own pattern as we live moral lives. When we sense others' needs or feel their despair, then we care about them and work to bring assistance when we can. When we assist or give to others without receiving recognition for it, we are being Christ in their lives. When we define "success" as living happily as a member of God's family and not as having maximized our self-interest, then we are living righteously. Moral living is moving as God directs in obedience to his laws, in serving humanity, and honoring His creation.

When we recognize God's path for us and follow it, we are responding obediently to Him through moral living.

The Hebrews were obedient to God though they often didn't understand everything immediately. We all learn why we're to be moral—sooner or later.

" . . .The Lord our God we will serve,
and His voice we will obey!"
Joshua 24:24 (NKJV)

Spiritual virtues may be easier to separate from all other virtues, which lend themselves to the secular realm; however, we should look upon all virtues as spiritual ones. The Ten Commandments direct us in social contacts with others, in respect for our parents and others, in truthfulness and honesty in our relationships, and in obedience to God.

When we choose to do anything that isn't moral, then we've chosen to live at lower levels than God intended us to live.

God has given us choices, and we have the opportunity to decide at which level we are going to live our lives.

"Be kind and compassionate to one another
forgiving each other,
just as in Christ God forgave you."
Ephesians 4:32 (NIV)

Relationship skills make our lives easier every day. When we speak kindly to others, behave cooperatively and willingly, when we do our part of the chores cheerfully, and when all others can depend upon us—our lives are certainly easier. Our work is to assist our grandchildren in understanding this.

Not all children see the benefits possible for them if they behave compatibly within the group. If they often see adults who take advantage of others, speak unkindly about others who're not present, handle their affairs without concern for others and are openly greedy, then expecting them to live compatibly in their families or social groups is contradictory to all they ever see.

Children living in the presence of adults who have no relationship skills, and no interest in changing themselves, will grow up without these skills. These skills are seldom learned if they're not present in families. Resentment of those who get along with all others, as well as low self-esteem is the result for younger children. As they become older, they find their companions among others who are stricken by the same malady, often turning hard-hearted, mean, and distrustful—all because the adults in the household cared little about the examples they set for the children in the home.

"[Lord], make your ways known to me, teach me your paths. Set me in the way of your truth, and teach me."
Psalm 25:4 (The Jerusalem Bible)

Through families God protects and guides children. Family is central to the larger community in the Old Testament, and the fifth Commandment demands honor for both mother and father, even though families at that time and for many centuries were patriarchal. The wisdom of the book of Proverbs teaches that respect is due equally to both mother and father.

In the New Testament, we find the church as it was first being established was often developed around family groups, whose members were significant Believers. As family members, they upheld their Christian beliefs—many times under great pains of the suffering and hardship dealt to the early Christians.They behaved as a unit, a family.

In the book of 2 Samuel we find *"The Lord declares to you that He will make you a house."* David had visions of building a great temple for God, but in these verses God is referring to family—the progeny of David, which includes Jesus.

The family group is not an insignificant entity. In all we do, say, or think about our families, we should remember God instituted families.

When we think of the family unit—the composition of it and and not the individuals making up the unit—as God's design, and as sacred work by God, then our relationship to each other is different and special within the family group. Can we live our lives within families just as God's people did in the Bible? We often tell our children to do things they don't understand; then later they do understand why they were to do as we directed them. This is the way the early Hebrews lived, *they trusted God.*

"I have no greater joy than to hear that my children are walking in the truth."
3 John 4 (NIV)

Sociologists, historians, psychologists and others define the family's role as being that of teacher and exemplar, the protector, and the provider. When children live in families whose daily lives are guided by God, and when they respond to Him through their love and search for His wisdom in all they do, then the essential requirements for parents and family are met without demands, definitions, and details being drawn.

Certainly there will be understanding, loving, forgiving, accepting, healing, sharing, caring, helping, crying, laughing—all the movements of God as He is in us and we in Him. We may teach our grandchildren that they live in a spiritual universe, where God is available, creating, loving, understanding—and more. We may help them understand what this means to our family and to each individual in it. Lets work with them to carry these parts of our faith into the world to friends, our community, the larger world, and to all God's creation.

We Give to Friends; We Receive From Friends

"A friend loves at all times . . "
Proverbs 17:17 (NKJV)

"A man who has friends must himself be friendly."
Proverbs 18:24 (NKJV)

Thomas Moore wrote, *Next to family, perhaps the most important value of the soul is friendship.* Friends are very special people, and the relationship of friendship is also special and unique. Nothing is like it. Friends are people whom we love just as they are, sometimes loving them because they are so very different from us. We see them, and accept them, and we love them without conditions, willing to wrap them in compassion and understanding in all occasions.

Through friendship we learn benevolence and goodwill, and we learn the value of inducing these emotions throughout other relationships. Also, from friendship we may learn to love ourselves better.

"Let each one examine his own work, and then he will
have rejoicing in himself alone, and not in another.
For each one shall bear his own load."
Galatians 6:4,5 (NKJV)

"If you want to be respected by others,
the great thing is to respect yourself"
Fyodor Dostoyevsky (1821-1881)

Friends teach each other to pay attention and to accept any differences between them. Augustine Hippo (354-430 CE) said *true friendship is one soul in two bodies.* Life's most difficult lessons about forgiveness are often learned in the relationship between friends. Individuals often become friends of our entire family as we bring them into our homes, sharing our comfortable refuge with them and permitting them to learn more about us through our siblings and parents, the trappings and activities of our abodes.

Friendships take time and energy. Anytime, anywhere the hearts of two souls meet and feel need and response, it is then that caring, openness, and friendship may result.

The amazing gift of friendship is truly God directed,
for the dedication, trust, and emotional involvement
required to grow and maintain true friendship
is potentially costly and demanding.

We are placed in this life on Earth as God's relational people, and our responsibility is to be hospitable to all and to develop and maintain friendships with those of like minds. To all we should be kind, compassionate, and hospitable, always trying to reflect God to them.

In all we do with our grandchildren, in listening to them about their friends, in discussing what friendship is, in attending the events and ceremonies of their friends, and in being friend to their friends, we are doing the work of God in the world. In this, sharing our faith with our grandchildren becomes very easy and fulfilling for us.

Our World, Our Neighbors, Ourselves

" I tell you the truth, whatever you did
for one of the least of these brothers of mine,
you did for me."
Matthew 25:40 (NIV)

"Relation and community are not somewhere and sometime
but
everywhere and always."
Ralph Waldo Emerson (1803-1882)

Helping others doesn't require that we are steadily on a mission. By paying even slight attention to others instead of always to ourselves we stumble upon many opportunites to serve others. Jesus' story of the good Samaritan reports just such an occasion. Read this familiar passage (Luke 10:29-37) and look for the challenge faced by this Samaritan. Are we willing to serve when the opportunity arises and need is obvious? How do we show our grandchildren to serve when we wait for a convenient time to assist, or help only those on the list composed by our social club, or take food only to members of our church?

We're Divinely directed to look upon others
not as whose color, creed, or race is different,
but as God's people,
who are the same as I in God.

We're to look upon each other as God's creation, just as we are. When I say I am God's person, so are all other "I's" His people. Delaying our obligation to help others—for it is an obligation for persons of God—is the same as refusing to serve. Putting anything off to the future is futile, for the future never comes. But we do have *now*. Live in the *now*, do for *now*, care about *now*. Let's free our minds and our lives from working and doing for tomorrow; we will do today.

"Ora et labora."
"Prayer and labor work."
A Benedictine motto

Our concept of community began in our relationship with our childhood friends. They affirmed our desire to find love and kindness outside our families and provided us with even more than these. People of the Old Testament established themselves as a community in response to divine directives. They developed their family life and community life as one in response to God's will for them. Jesus' lessons taught oneness of all people through God's presence in each of us.

We are all God's people; and God is universal. When we teach these truths to our grandchildren, they may become troubled about news notices which no longer jar our souls. The pain,suffering, and dislocation of the children of Kosovo and the Sudan may truly disturb them. Are we disturbed that these persons are suffering so profoundly?

Young children often are attuned to the spiritual concerns of the world much more than are the adults around them. Adults may learn empathy and true love from little ones in their families. Can we see these situations through our grandchildren's eyes?

"We can be truly compassionate
when 'the other' ceases to be 'other.'"
Henri J. Nouwen

We do not need so much instruction;
we need only to be frequently reminded.

On July 30, 1619, in Virginia, the First Representative Assembly held in America met in a church to make decisions regarding the young colony. *"Be it for as men's affaires doe little prosper where God's service is neglected, all Burgesses took their place in the Quire till a prayer was said by Mr. Burke that it would please God to guide and santifie all our proceedings to His own glory and the good of this plantation."*[2]

Our nation began as a land of religious refuge. The founding fathers never neglected to allow for religious freedom, and the Constitution pronounces a division between government and religion whereas government may not interfere with the individual's faith.

We are happy to be in our country where we are able to worship when, if, and how we prefer, and we should announce our gratitude exhuberantly periodically. Thanksgiving seems a proper time for this, although churches and family groups might rejoice in religious freedom through other celebrations. We may remember the trials and hardship of the Puritans and other early colonists through ceremony annually. Eulogies to these forgotten ones, ceremony to help us remember again, memorials to our ancestors, thanksgiving for freedom of religion, songs of praise to God for years of care, all these would carry our grandchildren's generation forward by looking back in gratitude.

"We are what [God] has made us,
created . . . for good works,
which God prepared beforehand to be our way of life."
Ephesians 2:10 (NRSV)

"Everything that serves humanity and helps in
the activities of the world is rightly seen
as a divine activity."
Annie Besant (1847-1933)

Annie Besant became known over the world for her work with wayward children and homeless girls. She also worked with the people of India, helping them gain independence.[3] There are many whom we never knew but who helped us and many others through their care and compassion for the needy and powerless.

People are assisted in many ways, and we may participate in various ways to help those needing help. Prayers and secret caring for others, the philanthropy and gigantic gifts provided by companies and foundations, the compassion held by entire congregations for the sick and dying, all are related to God's presence in our hearts.

We receive when others receive, though these blessings may not be overtly felt by us. When the needy of our human family are assisted in any way by caring people, we feel the healing, the caring, the feeding.

William James in 1902 wrote, *"As regards prayers for the sick, if any medical fact can be considered to stand firm, it is that in certain environments prayer may contribute to recovery, and should be considered as a therapeutic measure. Being a normal factor of moral health in the person, its omission would be deleterious."*[4] Prayer for the sick, and healing through prayer are mentioned frequently in the Bible and have beena part of religious practice throughout recorded history.

During his ministry John Wesley wrote in his journal (which was published in 1909-1911) *"there is no holiness but social holiness. . . and to turn Christianity into a solitary religion is to destroy it."* As Christians we are directed to social service.

"He restores my soul;
He guides me in paths of righteousness."
Psalm 23:3 (NIV)

God guides us, restores us, leads us, renews and revives us, refreshes us. Knowing this gives us peace, joy, comfort. We can pray for God's renewing, restoring, guiding power for ourselves and all who are bereft in any way in their lives.

Teaching our grandchildren to find God's power through the Bible, study and prayer, and to project it to others through prayer may lead to blessings of great magnitude in the world.

In Matthew we are told to do to others as you would have them do to you; and in Hebrews the writer suggests it would be good to be hospitable to strangers—just in case we might be entertaining angels without knowing it. Both are sound bits of advice if we're doing good as part of a deal, but if we are following the words of Jesus and we're representing God in the world, we are doing good because we're supposed to do it, without expecting recognition or repayment in any form. Donald Walsh questions whether we should perform good deeds as a response to need because we all like so much to feel needed. *The greatest gift you can give someone is the strength and the power not to need you, to need you for nothing.*[5]

"It is Christ in his distressing disguise
whom I love and serve."
Mother Teresa of Calcutta

Our grandchildren will respond to serving just as we respond. The very best we can do for them is to walk humbly with God, to love our neighbor—near and far—as ourselves, and to treat all others as we would like to be treated. That is all we have to do, for ourselves and for our grandchildren. And Yes! We do receive when we give.

God's World of Natural Wonders

"Mountains and hills will break into joyful cries
before you
and all the trees of the countryside clap their hands."
Isaiah 55:12 (The Jerusalem Bible)

"Glance at the sun.
See the moon and the stars.
Gaze at the beauty of
earth's greenings.
Now,
Think."
Hildegard of Bingen, 12th Century German Mystic

Most people are drawn to and inspired by nature. The Bible is filled with its abounding glory. The Psalms speak of elements of nature, Jesus referred to it in many of his parables, and we see the Hebrews living out their lives in the wilderness. Poets are struck by the breadth and depth of nature and respond in words that make our hearts sing.

"It is the first mild day of March
Each minute sweeter than before . . .
There is a blessing in the air . . ."
William Wordsworth (1770-1850)

Thomas Moore in *The Re-Enchantment of Everyday Life* writes for us, *Nature feeds the spiritual life like nothing else can—we need simple proximity, contemplation, ritual, and a spirit of piety. If we can allow ourselves to be stunned by nature's beauty, complexity, simplicity, devastating power, vast dimensions, and unexpected quirkiness, then lessons in spirituality will pour into us without effort on our part."*[6]

Children easily become caught up in the world of natural things. They bring us gifts of dandelion bouquets, broken acorns, crumpled leaves, plain old rocks, crickets dead and alive—all of them fascinanting treasures. How many frogs have we found on their toy shelves, with their eyes bulging as we spy them resting in a plastic cup with a baggie covering it? How many ants, June bugs, spiders and other creepy-crawly things have we laundered in their jeans' pockets?

Children are naturally drawn to God's natural world.

Children are at home in the out-of-doors. The shyest little boy, the prissiest tiny girl, almost all are comfortable with nature. Nature feeds their imaginations. They miss little around them, and are more trusting than we amidst the weeds, insects, hot sun, cold wind, rain, snow, and all condtions and creatures. They receive pleasure from their experience with God's natural world—as God intended.

Our responsibility in helping our grandchildren experience God's outside world is minimal: we need only to take them outside. Our responsibility to ourselves is to take advantage of our grandchildren's excitement and optimism, their awe and worship and all else they provide us when we're outdoors together.

In the natural world we learn about progression, evolution, change, growth, disease, death, birth, reproduction, hope and promise—all included in God's plan for us. Children who are connected to nature by living in the country, having pets, or taking frequent outside ventures are regularly incorporating God's natural plan into their minds. Then when we discuss this with them, they will already be involved and will follow through with us about God's plan for them.

". . .Holy, holy, holy is the Lord of hosts;
The whole earth is full of His glory!"
Isaiah 6:3 (NKJV)

"Connection is what makes life bearable
for us humans."
Mary Pipher (Another Country)

Nature touches so much of our lives, lending knowledge and wisdom, recreation and inspiration. It connects us to God and to others in our lives. Our misfortune is that we don't set time aside to receive these gifts and be helped by them. Nor do we set aside our plans (which are frequently much different than God's plans for us) when we do spend moments in God's natural world. Our minds are on the material. Whether we take time to appreciate the world about us or to learn from it and grow, or never think about it—we as humans are responsible for its care. In Genesis we're informed that God put man in charge of all about him. What does this mean? Do we care? What happens when we don't care? What do we teach our grandchildren about man's responsibility to nature?

"The message of Providence (that God will take care
of us, ie Matthew 6:33) demands
something very great of man:
that he should make the care of
God's kingdom the prime care of his life." [7]
Romano Guardini

Is it our responsibility to instruct our grandchildren about the care of God's world? By doing so, we help them advance in faith and in wisdom. Sharing our faith with them also helps them maintain proper relationships within the family, with friends, in their communities, and in the larger world. Assuming responsibility to care for the natural world and accepting its frequent turbulance as well as it beauty, bounty, and its lessons of reproduction and death, teaches us about life and God's will for us.

"The true paradise is our world,
the world just as it is, with all its suffering,
but seen through the eyes that call it "very good."
Stephen Mitchell [8]

"O Lord my God, you are very great,
you are clothed with splendor and majesty.
[You] set the earth on its foundations; it can never be moved.
[You] make springs pour water into the ravines;
it flows between the mountains.
They give water to all the beasts of the fields.
[You] make grass grow for the cattle,
and plants for man to cultivate—
bringing forth food from the earth.
The moon marks off the seasons,
and the sun knows when to go down.
How many are your works, O Lord!
In wisdom you made them all."
Psalm 104:1,5,10,11,14,19,24 (NIV)

Activities for Chapter Five

Our times with our grandchildren are usually spent within the confines of the secular physical society, with all its materialism, its attractions, urges and temptations, and its busyness and noise.

Our purpose will be to move with our grandchildren into and through all this, learning, growing in wisdom, choosing courageously and with insight, and praying for God's guidance in all we choose to do.

The following activities will move you and your grandchildren about in the secular world, encouraging you to carry the message of God within your mind, your heart, speaking it from your mouth, and willing it through your actions of service and relational deeds.

By this time you will have devised many good projects yourselves. Please use them as well as the ones you choose here. Living our faith through service in the world keeps our grandchildren focused on others, study, the Bible, Jesus, God, and the church as they grow toward adulthood.

1. Discuss service to others and how it should be one of your daily goals. Ask your grandchildren to make a list of ten ways they may help someone. Not all of them need to be difficult and time-consuming. Saying "thank you" when someone does a simple favor or kindness for them, complimenting one whom they seldom speak to at school, telling their teacher they appreciate her help—all will make the recipients feel good. Have them add ideas for helping their parents or siblings; to help a neighbor; another to assist a club or church or community organization; and one to help them carry out their responsiblity to our natural world.

When their lists are completed, let them decide which they will do today, then tomorrow. As they do them, suggest that they begin to add others so their lists will have no ending. Our service to others never ends. If there are young brothers or sisters in the family, suggest they all help each other with their lists. At the end of the first week, plan a time to share with all the family how they feel about their services.

2. Help each grandchild make or buy a journal, or a notebook to be used as a journal. Discuss how journals are kept and encourage frequent updates so they'll realize their own growth along their spiritual paths in future months or years. Journals are not diaries, not the place for "I hate my brother" and information on the cutest boy in school. They are records of significant turns, achievements, disasters, or other outstanding events in our lives; or the record of a steady course through life. (Of course, "all A's" need to be recorded.) Journals may be written as full descriptive letters or simple notes and should always be dated accurately. Individual styles add flavor for readers at a later date.

Before your grandchildren begin their journaling, write a note in the front describing where you see your grandchild at this time, how special he is, what your hopes are for him, and other words you'd like to say. Write a prayer to God about your grandchild that you may pray frequently for him, and a couple of your favorite Bible verses or hymns.

Let your grandchild know that many other people all over the world write in journals, some writing prayers beseeching God to bring good to everyone in the world. We all benefit from these prayers.

Some people keep journals for many years. Frequently, when a journal writer dies, members of the family keep and cherish the journals which were written by the deceased. Talk about this with your grandchildren.

4. Plan a day to clean God's paths and roads. Ask friends to join your family group to pick up trash in a park or along a road which parents agree is safe enough for this activity. Provide enough plastic trash bags and water bottles for everyone. Invite all who helped to a picnic with sandwiches and cookies when you're finished, remembering to leave no trash in the park. Thank everyone before they leave, and encourage them to join you in being responsible inhabitants of God's earth.

5. Plan to visit a close friend and to take your grandchild with you. Before you go, tell him about the good times you've had together, how your friend has always been helpful and dependable, and how she has helped you many times when you couldn't help yourself. Describe emergencies you've gone through together, fun times you're shared, dinners and shows you've attended. Tell how funny or brilliant she is, where she's traveled and about her big garden. Make your friend come alive for your grandchild before you arrive at her home. Conversing in this way with him will make him feel he knows your friend—and you will be alive with great appreciation for her yourself.

Stop on the way and purchase a package of cookies,a magazine, or something you know your friend enjoys. Let your grandchild help you choose.

After the visit, invite your friend to visit you soon, planning a time when your grandchild may help you prepare for the occasion. On the way home, talk about the good visit you had. Discuss friendship and how valuable this relationship is for all of us.

6. When we perform solitary tasks—dusting, washing dishes, pulling weeds, ironing, mowing—we may silently pray as we do our work. Praying for peace on earth, for someone we know is hurting, for greater knowledge of God, or for attributes such as compassion and forgiveness connects us to God and lifts us as we labor. Practice this at least once each day and recommend it to your grandchildren. Suggest that as they wait for the bus, ride to school, do their chores at home, or anytime they find themselves alone and quiet, they may pray for themselves or others.

7. If you are associated with a church, discuss within the family how you may take on a family project to do something for others through the church. For older adolescent children, there may be projects in another country in which they may participate during school vacation. In our communities, our grandchildren may work with older people in nursing homes, with pre-school children at our church day care center, or help gather food for homeless people. Every church has long lists of helping programs in which adults and children may participate.

When we serve others, we grow in wisdom, strength and compassion as we use our time, energy and resources for people other than ourselves.

Note

Sharing our faith with our grandchildren will have become a part of our daily lives. People of God live their days in His light and find there's no greater effort needed to live as righteously as we're able than to resign oneself to the pits of secularization. Though we live in the world, we may do so with God's joy in our hearts and His purpose on our paths. With purpose in our lives we remain focused, and when our purpose is sharing our faith with our grandchildren, they and we are blessed.

"There are diversities of gifts, but the same Spirit.
There are differences of ministries, but the same Lord."
1 Corinthians 12:4-5 (NJKV)

" . . . the Spirit helps us in our weakness."
Romans 8:26 (NIV)

May God's love and strength be yours as you tread ever forward on your path.

Sources

FAITH

1. Martin Buber, quoted in *Spiritual Literacy: Reading the Sacred in Everyday Life* by Frederick and Mary Ann Brussat, (New York: Scribner, 1996), 497.
2. Robert Fulghum, *Words I Wish I Wrote*, (New York: HarperCollins Publishers, Inc., 1977), 166.
3. W.H. Auden, quoted in *Spiritual Literacy* by Brussat and Brussat, 152.

Chapter 1—**GOD**

1. Romano Guardini, *The Art of Praying*, (Manchester, New Hampshire: Sophia Institute Press, 1985), 10.
2. Bill Moyers, *Genesis*, quoted by Professor Samuel Proctor, (New York: Doubleday, 1996), 144.
3. Kathleen Norris, *Amazing Grace*, Catherine M. LeCugna quote, (New York: Riverhead Books, 1998), 109.
4. Romano Guardini, *The Art of Praying*, 41.
5. David Jeremiah, *Prayer, the Great Adventure*, (Orange, CA: Mulnomah Publishers, 1977).
6. J.I. Packer, quoted in *Enter His Gates*, by Charles Stanley, (Nashville: Thomas Nelson Publishers, 1998), 324.

Chapter 2—**JESUS**

1. David Jeremiah, *Prayer, the Great Adventure*, 36.

Chapter 3—**THE HOLY BIBLE**

1. George Muller, quoted in *Halley's Bible Handbook*, (Grand Rapids: Zondervan Publishing House, 1965), 4.
2. *Webster's New World Dictionary*, (New York: Simon and Schuster, Inc. 1988).
3. Billy Graham, *The Faithful Christian*, quoted in *Let Faith Change Your Life* by Becky Tirabassi, (Nashville: Thomas Nelson Publishers, 1997), 113.
4. *Halley's Bible Handbook*, 50-57.
5. *The Wall Chart of World History*, drawn by Professor Edward Hull, (London: Studio Editions, Ltd., 1988).
6. *Oxford Companion to the Bible*, edited by Bruce M. Metzger and Michael D. Coogan, (New York:Oxford University Press, 1993), vi.
7. Owen Chadwick, *A History of Christianity*, (New York, St Martin's Press, 1995), 208-9.
8. Owen Chadwick, *A History of Christianity*, 208.
9. Ibid., 45, 47.
10. Ibid., 178, 181.

11. Ibid. , 178-180.
12. *The Reader's Encyclopedia,* edited by William Rose Benet, (New York: Thomas Crowell Co., 1955), 972,1180.
13. *The Oxford Companion to the Bible,* 619.
14. The American Bible Society, 1865 Broadway, New York, NY 10023.
15. John Allegro, *Dead Sea Scrolls,* (New York: Penguin Books, 1956, Second revised edition, 1964).

Chapter 4—**WE WORSHIP GOD**

1. Romano Guardini, *The Art of Praying,* (Manchester, New Hampshire: Sophia Press, 1985), 41.
2. James Hillman, *The Soul's Code,* (New York: Random House, 1996).
3. Kathleen Norris, *Amazing Grace,* 151.
4. Romano Guardini, *The Art of Praying,* 91.
5. *Oxford Companion to the Bible,* 665.
6. Kathleen Norris, *Amazing Grace* .
7. *Webster's New World Dictionary*
8. A.N. Wilson, *Paul, the Mind of the Apostle,* (New York: W.W. Norton, 1997).
9. Thomas Moore, *The Re-Enchantment of Everyday Life,* (New York: HarperCollins Publishers, Inc., 1996), 309.
10. Reader's note to the "Mailbox" Department; Alexandra Kennedy, Editorial Director, (Boone, IA: *Family Fun,* April, 1997), 14,16.
11. Lancelot Andrews, 1555-1626, included in *The Doubleday Prayer Collection* compiled by Mary Batchelor, (New York: Doubleday Publishing Co., 1992, 1996), 272.

Chapter 5—**LIVING OUR FAITH IN THE WORLD**

1. William Bennett, *The Book of Virtues,* (New York: Simon & Schuster, 1993).
2. Copied from an inscription on a bronze plaque in Bruton Parish Church, Williamsburg, Virginia, October, 1998.
3. *The Reader's Encyclopedia,* 101.
4. William James, *Varieties of Religious Experience,* (New York: Collier Books, 1961).
5. Neale Donald Walsh, *Conversations with God, Book 2,* (Charlottesville, VA: Hampton Roads Publishing, 1997).
6. Thomas Moore, *The Re-Enchantment of Everyday Life,* 4-5.
7. Romano Guardini, *The Art of Praying.*
8. Bill Moyers, *Genesis,* quote by Stephen Mitchell.